THE GUIDE TO
GETTING
PAID

THE GUIDE TO
GETTING
PAID

WEED OUT BAD PAYING CUSTOMERS,
COLLECT ON PAST DUE BALANCES,
AND **AVOID** BAD DEBT

MICHELLE DUNN

WILEY

John Wiley & Sons, Inc.

Published by John Wiley & Sons, Inc., Hoboken, New Jersey.
Published simultaneously in Canada.

For general information on our other products and services or for technical support,
please contact our Customer Care Department within the United States at
(800) 762-2974, outside the United States at (317) 572-3993 or fax (317) 572-4002.

Wiley also publishes its books in a variety of electronic formats. Some content that
appears in print may not be available in electronic books. For more information about
Wiley products, visit our web site at www.wiley.com.

ISBN 978-1-118-01161-4 (cloth); ISBN 978-1-118-05848-0 (ebk);
ISBN 978-1-118-05847-3 (ebk); ISBN 978-1-118-05846-6 (ebk)

Printed in the United States of America.

10 9 8 7 6 5 4 3 2 1

This book is dedicated to my children, Nathan and Jonathan Linden.
Special thanks to Kevin, Josh, Harry, and Ron.

CONTENTS

FOREWORD

I was 12 years old in 1973 when my life was placed on a course that would prove to be both exciting and rewarding. My parents opened a collection agency in central Pennsylvania, and while my friends played in their backyards and later worked in local stores and amusement parks over summer vacations, I was emptying office trash cans, filing ledger cards, and stuffing mail in envelopes for the family business. My eyes were opened at an early age to the dynamics of credit, the importance of managing credit and collection processes, and the extent to which businesses can suffer enormous financial losses by failing to appreciate the need to manage the acquisition of new customers and the resulting payment for products and services.

Over the past 35 years, I have developed a career that's included an active role as a collection agency owner, as a college professor, as a nationally recognized trainer in the credit and collection industry, and as president of ACA International, the Association of Credit and Collection Professionals. I continue to embrace the notion that proper education is the very foundation of business success. For that reason, I am delighted to recommend, *The Guide to Getting Paid: Weed Out Bad Paying Customers, Collect on Past Due Balances, and Avoid Bad Debt,* as an essential source for anyone planning a business venture, entering corporate life as a credit and collection professional, or having aspirations to own and manage a business enterprise in the future.

I have known and respected Michelle Dunn's fine work throughout her extensive career in the industry as a business operator and author. She has made enormous inroads toward educating credit and collection industry professionals through her insightful publications, presentations at industry conferences and events, and one-on-one coaching of financial professionals. *The Guide to Getting Paid* is written from the perspective of an author who not only academically understands this industry's dynamics, but who has also applied the recommended strategies to her own company as well as to countless others. There have been many articles and books written over the years on the subject of credit and collections. While many of these are useful, this publication differs in that it presents valuable knowledge in a concise and clear format that allows the reader to easily develop the repertoire of skills necessary for financial business success. From the onset of the book—which outlines exactly what credit management is—through the chapters on How Credit Affects Businesses, Effective Payment Arrangements, Using E-Mail and Social Media for Collections, Choosing a Third Party Debt Collection Firm, and finally, Debt Collection Laws, Rules, and Regulations, Michelle creates a wonderful foundation for success for the eager and willing student.

Read on and prepare to absorb the many dynamics and nuances of the credit and collection industry. Open your mind to the recommendations that this subject matter expert makes as you embark on a position or career in any business office where your skills will directly impact the enterprise's financial success or failure. Congratulations on making the decision to join the hundreds of thousands of professionals that keep money flowing and bills current in today's business landscape. Reading Michelle Dunn's, *The Guide to Getting Paid: Weed Out Bad Paying Customers, Collect on Past Due Balances, and Avoid Bad Debt* is a surefire way to put your best foot forward for credit and collection success.

Harry A. Strausser III
President, Remit Corporation and
Interact Training & Development

* * * * *

Harry A. Strausser III, President, Remit Corporation, owns and manages Remit Corporation, a full-service third party debt collection firm in Bloomsburg, Pennsylvania. The firm specializes in medical receivables, commercial debt, and the purchase and management of accounts for debt buyers. Through the corporation's subsidiary, Interact Training & Development, he presents many programs annually throughout the United States and abroad on credit, collection, communication, and motivation. He has served for more than 16 years as an adjunct professor of communication at Bloomsburg University of Pennsylvania, where he has instructed in public speaking, interpersonal communication, and corporate communication. For more than 20 years he has maintained the status of Certified Trainer with ACA International Inc., the trade association of credit and collection professionals, during which he has presented hundreds of programs to industry professionals. He currently writes the Training Advisor column for Collection Advisor *magazine, a widely read trade publication in the credit and collection industry. When not traveling to speaking events he resides in Bloomsburg, Pennsylvania.*

PREFACE

I am writing this book because while most business owners have a business plan and even a marketing plan, very few have a credit plan. It should come as no surprise that cash is a company's biggest asset; therefore, failing to have a plan in place to protect that asset is one of the biggest mistakes businesses and entrepreneurs make. This book will help you understand what credit management and credit policies are, the objectives of a credit policy, and how it affects your business and customers. You will learn what affects your business's cash flow and how to manage it, and be able to write your own credit policy for your business and improve your bottom line using credit management.

More than 10,000 companies today have slow or nonpaying customers. This book will help these organizations collect the money they are owed efficiently and quickly and keep that money coming in. This book's goal is to teach readers how to take specific steps and use positive action to streamline and maximize your credit management policies. I offer step-by-step actions that business owners can take in order to weed out bad customers, increase your customer base with quality customers that pay on time, collect past-due balances, avoid bad debt, and increase profits using effective credit management techniques. This book includes techniques, tips, and procedures you can take in order to be profitable, increase your cash flow, and make more money from someone who has "been there and done that."

The Guide to Getting Paid will also help business owners obtain credit from lenders by incorporating a credit policy or plan into their existing business strategy. Company owners who approach lenders with a business plan have a pretty good chance of being considered for a loan; however, having a marketing plan and a credit policy as well increases their chances of obtaining that loan by more than 85 percent. A credit policy shows potential lenders how you will manage your cash, cash flow, limit your risk, how and when you will be paid, and what actions or steps you will take when you are not paid in order to recover those funds. In essence, providing a credit policy explains to the lender in detail how you will pay them back.

Here are some interesting statistics:

1. About 32 percent of business owners in 2010 complained that customers are taking more time to pay. That figure is up from 27 percent in 2008, according to a survey of more than 700 entrepreneurs taken by American Express OPEN, the company's small business division. About a third claim that they plan to improve cash flow by being more aggressive in collecting accounts receivables.

2. A study published by Jessie Hagan of U.S. Bank reveals that 82 percent of small businesses fail because they can't manage their money.

3. A recent Federation of Small Business survey of 1,400 members found that only 16 percent of businesses had approached the banks for credit, and a third of those had been refused (Published: August 20, 2010—John Walker, National Chairman, FSB).

This data highlights the fact that customers are still struggling to pay their bills on time; small business owners are still not educated on how to manage their cash flow; and banks are still holding back on extending credit. This book will help you to tackle all three of these problems and come out on top.

The Small Business Association noted in a recent briefing that entrepreneurship is crucial to the nation's economic revival and competitiveness in a global marketplace. Furthermore, an environment ripe for those with dreams of owning their own business, combined with the need for such new businesses to thoroughly understand financial practices, opens many doors for the entrepreneurially minded.

This book provides entrepreneurs and business owners with essential information on how to have an effective in-house credit policy that helps them make more sales, increase cash flow, and make a profit. Reading this book will allow you to take action to limit your credit risk and increase your bottom line immediately. By following the outlined steps, you will have a professional credit policy that you can take to your bank to help you get approved for loans and grow your business.

This book will help you to decide what is most important to you in regards to your customers, billing, payment terms, pricing, and cash flow. Being educated about these matters will allow you to implement procedures based on your own preferences and prioritize what will work for you, your business, your employees, your vendors, and your customers.

Credit management is the management of your business credit, accounts payable, and receivables. *The Guide to Getting Paid* will teach you how to do that in an efficient and effective way that will benefit your company and everyone who comes in contact with it. You will see how to determine the factors that are most important to you, and how to put these items in writing via an effective credit policy.

It is absolutely vital that your customers are aware of your credit policies and payment terms before they do business with you. Of course, all consumer interactions carry some level of risk. This book will teach you how to check and issue credit, determine credit risk, and various other ways to limit that risk. You will then learn how to put those steps into writing so that your employees or credit management department can effectively follow those procedures when you have a potential new customer.

This is the area that causes most business owners to pull their hair out. While writing your own credit policy sounds scary and difficult, this book will make it much easier, even painless. I have included real life examples and outlines that you can use for your own business. Many company owners are not familiar with the common mistakes made during credit management when they begin with a credit policy. Such mistakes include not checking credit, not getting any signed paperwork, being unfamiliar with laws, and more. This book will tell you exactly what those mistakes are, how to avoid them, and how to use that information to strengthen your cash flow and profits. In short, *The Guide to Getting Paid* will take the nightmare out of collections by helping you implement simple policies that will save you time, money, and headaches.

1

WHAT IS CREDIT MANAGEMENT?

If you own a business, you know that you occasionally have customers who owe you money—and that you sometimes struggle in your attempts to collect that money. You appropriately become frustrated with not getting paid after you complete a job. Perhaps you ship an order and then have to make collection calls, or maybe you just ignore the problem and hope the bill will eventually be paid.

Smart company owners learn how to collect the money that is owed them. They also know how to prevent accounts from becoming past-due, and how to keep their customers on track with less effort. That is what is called credit management.

Credit management is the process by which you control your business's credit, accounts payable, and receivables. Correctly managing your business's credit entails creating an outline of policies and procedures that will provide your customers with options when they cannot pay in full and on time. Effective credit policies provide an outline or plan that will enable you to adequately provide reasonable credit limits for customers who have revolving credit. This plan would also include procedures on how to deal with past-due or late-paying accounts, as well as advice on how to eliminate them from the books. You want to have guidelines to legally collect money owed to your company that has been lost due to late payers, nonpaying customers, and bad checks. You also want to establish a streamlined system that will maintain timely contact with all of your late-paying customers. These procedures help you to be aware of when accounts are becoming past-due and to help you avoid carrying bad debt on the receivables.

Business owners all have different types of companies in various industries, all of which can extend credit. Therefore, it should make sense that no two credit policies will be the same. One major difference is that which exists between a service or retail business. Your credit policy should use multiple facets to cater to prospective customers but also protect you and your organization.

You are limited in what you can and cannot ask a prospective customer in order to extend them credit. You need to be aware of what these questions and the associated laws are before you create your credit policy, which will help to filter customers so you don't have to spend your time chasing your money. The best credit policy is short, easy to understand, and to the point; it should avoid long-winded statements with a lot of legal terminology or big words. Always create your policy and forms with the customer in mind—the easier and the clearer, the better.

OBJECTIVES OF CREDIT MANAGEMENT

If you don't have a credit policy for your business, everyone will want to buy from you, which can result in unpaid and past-due invoices on your books. In order to be effective, your credit policy must meet the following objectives:

- Effectively outlines policies and procedures that will help provide your customers with options when they cannot pay in full.
- Implements a plan that will enable your business to adequately provide reasonable credit limits for your customers that have revolving credit accounts.

- Outlines the steps to take to collect from past-due or late-paying customers and how to eliminate bad debt.
- Provides guidelines to legally collect money that is due to your company from slow or nonpaying customers and from bad checks.
- Exacts a streamlined system to deal with any past-due accounts.

Once you've established your credit management policies or procedures, you will know how to maintain your cash flow to benefit you and your business—and how to get customers to pay easily and quickly. The longer you wait to take action on getting paid, the lesser your chances are of receiving any money. A credit management plan maintains your customers' satisfaction and insures reliable payment of accounts, and the credit policy sets a positive credit tone for your business. It also lets potential customers know that you are serious about your business, and lets you control your customers, cash flow, and profits.

It is up to you how tightly you wish to enforce your policy. You can have a very strict credit policy—which alienates some customers—or a looser policy if you are willing to take a bigger risk. Some business owners have more flexible credit policies for a variety of reasons. They may want to open several new accounts quickly, they might be a large market or a competitive industry, or they may offer less discriminating credit terms for a limited time to introduce a new service or product. Or they may simply have a large inventory in a warehouse and want to move it quickly.

Whatever your level of stringency, any successful in-house policy must:

- Be tough yet flexible
- Have specific action guidelines
- Be enforced consistently

Proper and regular attention involves developing a collection procedure or policy and following each step fully before moving on to the next step. It means that you never move backward or repeat a step in the hope of salvaging an account. You need to be firm with policy enforcement and attentive to your policy's details.

Good credit management is crucial to your business. If you can't manage the cash and credit that flows through your company, it will inevitably fail. You must respect your cash and deal with it properly in order to be successful.

Some business owners feel that it's easier to process orders just by obtaining limited information on the customers. Many new entrepreneurs are so excited to make the sale that they don't want to offend the customer by asking them to fill out a credit application. Their next mistake in this situation is not asking for the money when it is due. They were so thrilled to make the sale that they're afraid to anger the customer by asking for the money—even when it is past-due. They don't realize that this means that they actually *failed* to make the sale in the first place.

Take a different approach here by showing potential customers that you are proud of what you do and serious about your business by asking them to fill out a credit application. Any customer who takes offense to this or refuses to fill out the application is probably not creditworthy—and is one you wouldn't want as a customer anyway.

Most business owners don't realize that a credit policy is a method to control their bottom line, sales, and income. Using this tool to increase your sales and profits is a smart maneuver that many companies unfortunately ignore. A credit application a potential customer fills out provides near-perfect information about them and how they pay their bills. It also helps you decide if the customer can afford more credit.

Be warned that when you utter the word "credit," the first thing that comes to most people's minds is "bad." Credit has a variety of different meanings. This book focuses on both your company's and your customers' credit—a combination of which can sometimes result in debt. In fact, over 70 percent of American consumers that use credit cards have no idea what interest rates they are paying; that's a pretty scary fact!

Most people's credit problems are unexpected. People generally do not buy items on credit with the intention of not paying and just running off into the sunset (okay, maybe a few do). However, some of the most common causes of credit problems are:

- Unexpected medical bills
- Lack of savings
- No experience dealing with money or a budget
- Unemployment
- Overextending oneself financially
- Accidents or emergencies
- Separation and divorce
- Death of a spouse or other family member

Developing an understanding of the most common causes of credit problems will help you be more effective in trying to collect money that is due to you.

People use credit for many different things that range from quieting children to keeping up with the neighbors. Many consumers believe that the more credit you have, the more successful you are. For example, the platinum card makes us feel special, or a gold card means we are better or more successful than our neighbor who only has a silver card. A lot of people don't want to be limited by living within their means. They want more, and they want it now—and they are bringing their children up the same way. Someone who uses a credit card to fulfill that dream when they can barely make ends meet is essentially making a deal with the devil. However, you can help control this problem by assisting your customers in making the right choices. You can do this by limiting their credit to what they can afford, thereby benefiting both your customers and your business.

HOW CREDIT MANAGEMENT AFFECTS YOUR CUSTOMERS

Your credit management plan is a two-way street; you create the rules and your customers have to play by them if they want to do business with you. If your customers don't follow your rules, they are out of the game. It is your job to be fair, reasonable, and follow the law to ensure your customers will not be intimidated by your credit policy and will continue to be good paying customers who refer you to others.

Some customers with a history of bad credit look to buy specifically from companies where they don't have to fill out a credit application or any type of new account forms. Any customer who balks at filling out any new account information should be established as Cash on Delivery (COD) or prepayment only. Never extend credit without getting at least a signed credit application and checking references. A quality customer will not run away when they have to fill out any paperwork, and will be glad to see that they are dealing with an organized, professional business. They will feel more secure doing business with you and will appreciate how serious you are about keeping your company profitable. This elevates your organization in the customers' eyes; they will know you are an upstanding business owner with values and will want to continue to interact with you.

Extensive research found that consumers who can obtain credit will even pay more for a product or service when they are extended credit and have great customer service. Faster, easier, and smoother procedures will garner the most sales and better paying customers. The result is more transactions, more income, and happier customers. It can also prompt free and valuable word-of-mouth advertising from satisfied customers.

Knowing the types of customers you have can also help you to limit your credit risk. Your customer base can be compiled by many different types of people with different needs depending on the type of business you have. However, you should be aware of the following individuals, as they will almost surely put you at risk:

- *Slow payers* who are forgetful or unorganized.
- Those who *"want to pay but can't"* due to economic circumstances.

- Those who *are able to pay but unwilling* due to a dispute or complaint.
- *Credit criminals*: people who commonly apply for credit, then don't pay or find a reason not to pay.

Make sure the credit applications you give new customers are simple and to the point. Jamming too much stuff onto applications and forms scares away potential customers—especially if they can go somewhere else, fill out one easy form, and get the product or service they're seeking right away. Customers are distracted by long forms, especially those full of legal jargon, long technical terms, or that ask for too much information. Keep the forms short and the language easy to understand.

Customers, creditors, and business owners can assess your business's credibility based solely on your policies. If you extend credit without making sure the proper application is filled out, customers know you aren't serious, which could lead to collection issues down the road. The first step is to design a customer-friendly policy that ensures you have the information you need if there is ever a payment problem but also a policy that doesn't scare away your customers. You must maintain amicable customer relations while protecting yourself and your company from potential financial adversity. The second step is to make sure that the policy is in effect *before* obtaining new customers, and ensuring that everyone in your organization is familiar with and enforces your policy. It is not very professional to be searching for a credit application or not know which forms they have to fill out in order to open a new account.

If you come to realize that your credit application is not working for you—or you are having problems with some aspect of your credit policy—you can change it at any time and measure your results to be sure the new approach is an improvement. The best strategy for ensuring an effective credit policy is to look at your bottom line and talk to your customers. Are most of your credit-approved customers paying on time or are you extending credit to customers who are paying slowly or not at all? Are your customers having any problems or questions with the forms or the information they had to provide? Keep asking these questions; it will enable you to tweak your policy so that it is streamlined and working as efficiently as possible.

The following are some steps you can take to make your credit policy easy, quick, and painless.

- *Make it easy* for the customer to get credit with you. Have packets paper-clipped together at the front desk; include the credit application, automatic payment permission forms, and anything else you want filled out before opening an account. You can print out these forms and clip them together or put them in a clipboard and hand them to every new customer to fill out. Make it a policy of yours and your employees and you should never make an exception.
- *Make it quick* by having these packets ready and waiting for anyone who comes in. Have pens and clipboards available so the forms can be filled out immediately.
- *Make it painless* by either having them wait and checking their credit application while they are present or

responding to them within a certain time period, say 24 hours.

Like everyone else, consumers today expect convenience and speed. You risk losing a customer if you make the account-opening process too difficult or unorganized.

ELEMENTS THAT AFFECT CREDIT MANAGEMENT

It is important that your customers know your credit policies and payment terms before they begin interacting financially with you. Reiteration of your credit policy and procedures when payment is overdue is a good step to take in trying to obtain payment. Once you extend credit, it is important to maintain accurate records on an account's payment history—and always adhere to your collection policies, no matter what events transpire. You cannot predict the future or changing market conditions. To anticipate economic fluctuations, try to keep current with trade reports pertaining to specific companies and industries. And *always* ask for payment when it is due. You should have procedures in writing for your employees as well as your customers; you might even consider framing a copy of the procedures and hanging it in your lobby or waiting room.

Customers who are approved for credit will buy more if they can pay later, so make the process as streamlined as you can. Another option is to advertise a free gift, in the same way that banks might offer an incentive such as a free toaster or blanket when you open a new checking account. Consider providing something such as a discount for credit-approved customers in a certain time frame. For example, "Get

25 percent off your first order if you apply for a credit account and are credit-approved between January 1 and January 14." It's a good idea to offer this type of deal to existing customers as well.

You only need credit management or a credit policy if you extend credit and your customers keep coming back. A good idea is to take a look at your competition and get an idea of what they do for credit-approved customers. Do they have a credit policy? If they do, what is included in it? What does their credit application look like and how long does it take them to process? You can find most of these answers online, since many businesses post this information on their websites.

WHAT IS CREDIT RISK?

Credit risk is the hazard of loss due to a default on a contract, or more generally, due to some "credit event." This has traditionally only applied to situations where debt holders or business owners were concerned that the debtor or customer to whom they made a loan or extended credit might default on a payment. For that reason, credit risk is sometimes also called default risk.

Almost all companies carry some credit risk, because most organizations do not demand upfront cash payments for all products delivered and services rendered. Instead, they supply the product or service and then bill the customer, often specifying their terms of payment. Credit risk is the time between when the customer receives the product or service and when you get paid.

Businesses were asked in a recent *Wall Street Journal* poll by icsolutions.com, "Are your customers taking more time to pay for your companies' goods and services?" Seventy-eight percent said yes, and 23 percent said no—results that clearly indicate an increase in customers paying with less speed. This is precisely why it is so crucial that you learn how to limit your business credit risk so that you can survive while customers take longer to pay.

WAYS TO LIMIT YOUR CREDIT RISK

The following are a few tactics you can employ to decrease your chances of running into problems in this area.

Invest in Education

Continue to educate yourself and your employees about the latest events in your industry. Attend seminars, free online webinars or tele-seminars; read books and trade magazines; and keep up to date on what is happening in your industry. Learn all that you can through whatever means are available to you.

Network and Make Contacts Online and Offline

Networking will keep you on everyone's minds. This way, if you end up losing your job you will have a slew of business cards of others in your field that you can contact during tough times.

Follow the Market

Read the newspapers or watch the news. Be aware of what is happening—both within your industry and in general—and stay on top of it.

Pay Off Debt

If you can pay off any debt, now is the time to do it. Dealing with a recession is hard enough without a boatload of debt to cause your stress level to go through the roof. Pay cash for anything you need. If you don't have the cash, ask yourself if you really *need* it or just *want* it. Try not to use credit cards (unless you pay them off in full each month) until you fully establish your company in order to build up your business credit.

Cut Back on Extras

This might seem like a simple suggestion until you really think about what it entails. For example, do you need all the bells and whistles you have on your business phone? Do you need a coffee service in your office or can you buy a coffee pot and brew your own much cheaper? Can you bring a bag lunch or carpool to work? There are countless ways to save a little here and a little there.

Build Your Online Presence

Create a website, blog, newsletters, or articles. Join online net-working groups that relate to your industry. Mentor someone or find a mentor for yourself or your business.

Have Your Clients or Customers Sign a Long-Term Contract

This is always a good idea. Or, another option, review existing contracts and either renew or extend them.

Specialize in Something

Make yourself and your company known as the experts or go-to people for a particular area of service. This will highlight your value, and employers are more likely to keep an employee who can do more than one thing.

You might find yourself with more time or feeling frustrated that you can't make more sales when business is low. Take that time as an opportunity to follow what's going on in the market. Read newspapers or watch the news, know what is happening with the economy, and stay aware of the latest developments. You'll relieve your frustration and improve your ability to forecast events that affect your business as you become more educated. Now is also the time to network and make sure your business stays on everyone's mind. Make contacts on- and offline to bring in more sales.

The following are some top tips to help you limit your credit risk.

- Give out as little credit as possible at the risk of losing sales (after all, bad credit risks aren't always worth the sale if you don't get paid).
- If you are going to extend credit, think like a banker; figure out exactly how you're going to be paid back.
- Remember that time is of the essence; get paid sooner rather than later.
- Have the facts in front of you before making a collection call.
- Be willing to negotiate.
- Hire a collection agency. (This is covered in more detail in Chapter 8, Third Party Collection Services.)

MANAGING CREDIT RISK

Managing credit risk is important for any company but especially for new or small businesses. Larger companies may have the advantage of a credit risk department whose job it is to assess customers' financial health and extend credit (or not) accordingly, much like a credit manager. For example, a new business that is selling its products to a troubled customer may attempt to lessen risk by tightening payment terms from "net 30" to "net 15," by actually selling less product on credit to the retailer, or even by cutting off credit entirely and demanding payment in advance. The business might lower the existing credit limit and rerun the credit application to reevaluate the credit risk factors. Though this might cause friction in the customer relationship, the company will be better off taking this approach with customers who are late in paying their bills. This is certainly the case if clients default and you have to place the account for collection, if you have to take them to court, or if they file bankruptcy.

On the other hand, credit risk is not really manageable for very small companies with only one or two customers. This makes these companies very vulnerable to defaults or even payment delays by their customers. If a business with only two or three customers hasn't limited their risk, they could find themselves unable to pay bills or get paid if just one of those customers is late in making a payment or goes out of business. This is an area in which it's particularly important not to put all your eggs in one basket. Establishing a broader customer base can help you extend credit while limiting your risk and managing your cash flow.

Some things you can do to limit your risk with existing customers are:

- Get a personal guarantee
- Offer month-to-month credit
- Offer ship-to-ship credit
- Ask for a security deposit to keep in a trust account in the event the customer does not pay an invoice
- Get a 50 percent deposit on every order and make sure the balance is paid upon order completion

The best approach here is to make sure that you get to know your customers as well as possible. In order to limit your risk but make your credit policy effective, you need to implement a procedure for any new or credit-approved existing customers. You should learn what your customers are looking for when they apply for credit with your company. It's simply good business to cater to potential new customers; the easier you make it for them to spend more money with you, the more money and sales you acquire.

You want to take steps to minimize your exposure to high-risk debt to limit your credit risk. You may have noticed that many banks and lenders have established much stricter guidelines recently for applying and being approved for credit lines than in the past. Bankruptcies are expected to continue to soar in the coming year, and revolving credit is becoming much harder to obtain. Revolving credit is a type of credit that does not have a fixed number of payments. An example of revolving credit is a credit card as opposed to a car loan, which would have a fixed number of payments.

Some things you can do to tighten your credit policy belt are:

- Be clear on the terms of your deal; get it in writing!
- If you extend credit, monitor the accounts for overdue payments, and keep them up to date.
- Have a penalty for past-due balances, such as a late fee or termination of credit privileges.
- Research collection agencies before you need one.
- Have every customer sign a credit application and *check their credit*—thoroughly!

The following are questions to ask yourself about your delinquent customers in order to limit your credit risk:

- Are they in a position to pay in full?
- Will they be in a position to pay your bill in six months?
- What will you do if they can't pay you?
- How will you pay your bills if your customers are delinquent?

What is your next step when your customers cannot pay you because of a job loss or other economic effects? Make sure that you follow the laws in your state to collect the money that is owed to you, even when things get tough. Be aware of the parameters in the Fair Debt Collection Practices Act (FDCPA) and treat your customers as you would like to be treated. Be sure to follow these rules, no matter how frustrated or upset you get.

- Do not berate or belittle the customer.
- Do not swear, yell, or use foul language.

THE GUIDE TO GETTING PAID

- Do not call and then hang up on a customer.
- Do not post a notice in your office or store that some customers owe you money.
- Do not extend them any more credit until they pay you, and afterwards always get cash up front.

CHECKING PEOPLE'S CREDIT

Let's say that you have a new customer who wants to apply for credit. You must first check their credit in order to make an educated decision on how much credit you want to extend to them, or how much of a risk you want to take in terms of what you extend to them. If you have signed up with a credit reporting agency to pull credit reports, then run a credit report once you've received the customer's application. You also will want to check all references. Even though most people list references that they know are good, you should check them all anyway. Make notes right on the credit application or new account form. Call the business, personal, and bank references, and always get the full name, title, and extension of the person giving the reference. Some questions you can ask during this process are:

- How long have you known the customer?
- How long has the customer been doing business with you?
- What payment method does the customer normally use?
- Does the customer generally pay within terms, late, or early to take a discount?
- What is the customer's average balance? How many days past-due is it (if any)?

- What is the average amount of the customer's orders?
- How often does the customer order from you?
- What is the customer's current balance due? Is any of that past-due? If yes, how many days past-due?
- What are the customer's terms with you?
- Does the customer make a lot of returns?
- Does the customer take any discounts?
- What is the customer's high amount of credit in the last year or six months? Have their orders increased or decreased in dollar amounts?
- Is the customer's account current today?

When you contact the bank for a reference, you sometimes will have to fax your request on your company letterhead stating that you have authorization from the customer to request the credit reference information. You can do this easily and give the bank a call afterwards to ask questions such as:

- What type of account does this person have—business, personal, savings, checking, business loan?
- When did the person open the account?
- What is the average daily balance?
- Has the person had any insufficient funds or other returned checks? How many? When was the last one?
- Does the customer have any outstanding loans?
- What types of loans does the customer have? Are they secured or unsecured? Are they being paid as agreed?

Many new and small business owners or credit managers are reluctant to run a credit report because of the cost involved. However, you need to think of this amount in relation to what you could lose by *not* pulling the report and checking credit. The cost to run a credit report as a member of a credit bureau is an investment that is well worth it.

When checking credit and looking at someone's existing debt to decide if they can afford more, keep the following figure in mind: a total personal debt should not exceed 36 percent of a person's total income. Remember this when checking people's credit.

Unfortunately, many folks nowadays have bad debts or are financially overextended. Common financial education is nonexistent unless your parents taught you about finances when you were a kid. Though issues pertaining to debt and bills are really common sense, it's not something that is taught in schools or colleges. However, the recent recession has shown us how important these lessons are, and young people these days must learn them in order to strengthen our economy.

WHAT TO AVOID WHEN EXTENDING CREDIT

While extending credit can seem intimidating at first, it doesn't have to be. This scary element comes from the fact that you put your business out on a limb when you extend credit; you're essentially hoping that whoever you're taking on will really pay you when they promise to. Here is a list of some things to watch out for when you are considering extending credit to a customer—new or old. Avoid extending credit when:

- Someone has no credit; offer another option such as 50 percent down, balance due upon delivery.

- Someone has bad credit; try COD or prepay.
- Someone cringes at filling out or signing any paperwork.
- Someone doesn't have a job.
- Someone doesn't have a permanent address and/or phone number.
- Someone asks to have another person, such as a cosigner, make the application.
- The applicant doesn't have a bank account.
- The applicant won't give you references.
- A check has been returned or a credit card denied.

These are just some of the red flags to look out for. When you extend credit, you put your business at risk; you therefore need to limit that risk as much as possible. You don't have to extend credit to everyone who walks through the door; plenty of your customers will be approved. So choose wisely and do your research in order to reduce your risk, and make more money.

UNDERSTANDING DEBT AND BAD DEBT

Debt is an obligation or promise to pay something on a certain date and by a certain time. It is what is owed to anyone who has extended credit to someone that has not been paid. Bad debt is what happens when someone doesn't pay their bills; it can result in their utilities being shut off or cancelled, repossession of big-ticket items like homes and cars, late fees, and being placed for collection or having to go to court.

Business owners all sell products or provide services with the understanding that customers will pay their bills. Companies that offer credit do this so they can make more money by extending credit to customers so that those people can afford their products or services. However, they lose money when those customers don't make their payments. Failing to make an agreed-upon payment after a business owner does you the courtesy of extending credit (a privilege) is disrespectful. Situations like these can cause both customers and businesses a lot of stress; customers aren't making their payments, and businesses are not getting paid—and in most cases, don't know why.

Did you know? Americans spend more than 70 percent of their gross income every year on repaying debt.

Bad debt is that which a customer has incurred and that is no longer collectible. It is therefore worthless to the creditor or business that extended the credit. Bad debt occurs once all avenues to try and collect a debt have been explored and proven unsuccessful. It can take place under a variety of circumstances; for example, when a customer files bankruptcy, dies, or skips town. It might also come about because the cost of trying to collect that debt is more than the actual debt. In these cases, the debts are normally written off to bad debt as an expense. Bad debt is normally expensed on the accounts ledger as a cost of doing business.

Though you will increase your sales as you sell on credit more often, you must make sure each customer is credit-worthy. Any bad debts that you write off will reduce your net income. However, most companies have a bad debt allowance since it is unlikely that all of their credit-approved customers will pay them in full.

One thing that many company owners frequently overlook is how to prevent future credit issues that normally result in bad debt. I am always amazed at how creditors will hire someone to collect the bad debts they have—and then do nothing to avert future problems. It is never too late to implement a credit policy, even if you have a pile of bad debt. And the sooner you do it, the better your chances are of collecting what is already owed to you and preventing future bad debts—thereby preventing the same situation from happening again.

According to collection trends, surveys, and polls taken— as well as from my own personal experience—every debt's chance of recovery drops drastically the longer it is allowed to be past-due. The more time you let a debt sit there, the harder it becomes to collect. This was one of the reasons I charged a higher commission on any debt over one year old when I had my collection agency. Regardless of the dollar amount, the older it is, the harder it is to collect—that is, *if* you manage to collect anything at all. Many business owners either don't know or don't understand this. I have watched countless proprietors leave debts on their books for years. They assumed their customer would pay when they had the money, and avoided contacting them so as not to make them angry. After they got sick of looking at it on their books, they would place the account with my agency—and never understood why they had to pay a higher commission. Perhaps this explanation will save you from making the same mistake. Now you know that if you aren't going to actively pursue your past-due accounts, you can't let them just sit on the books. Place them with an agency right away and you will get more of your money in the long run. Another approach: If you have a large amount of bad debt, you may want to think about offering a discount if someone pays cash at the time of sale, thereby protecting yourself and saving your customer money.

In 2008 the *Wall Street Journal* reported that bad debts have led to a change in billing—a trend that is prompting hospitals to demand cash up front from their patients. Traditionally, hospitals bill patients after they receive their care. However, with increased bad debt and charity care costs these days, hospitals want money before patients get treated. According to the American Hospital Association, unpaid bills for care given ended up costing the hospital industry $31.2 billion in 2006.

CREATING A CREDIT POLICY

When a new or potential customer asks to begin doing business with you, you should set up their account on a prepaid or cash only basis. You can then give or send the customer a credit application if they wish to become a charge customer. Once you receive the completed application, you need to check their credit and decide upon on a credit limit. If you approve the customer, you must send them a letter letting them know they have been approved, and for how much. You also have to notify them via letter if they were denied, and let them know what the reasons are. There must be a notation on the bottom of the letter telling them where they can call or write to obtain a free copy of their credit report if they disagree with any of the information.

Take the following specific steps to ensure successful credit management:

- Have every new customer fill out a credit application and/or new account form.
- Check customers' credit, and deny or approve in a timely manner.

- Send out a denial or approval letter.
- Lock all credit forms and information in a file cabinet to which only the owner or credit manager has a key. This information is confidential and should not be available to anyone else in your company.
- Input credit limits into your computer on customers' accounts.

There are several powerful strategies that business owners can use to dramatically improve their sales, income, and bottom line. One of these is to increase awareness within your organization about your credit policy. If just one department or person doesn't abide by your written credit policy, it can completely fall apart.

A second strategy is to put one person in charge of all credit applications and new account information. All of the material you obtain on a new customer is extremely confidential. For this reason, just one employee should be handling the processing of all the new account forms and credit applications, which should also be kept in a locked file cabinet.

Speed and convenience are other important issues. Consumers today are looking for fast, easy answers. The more efficient you can make your credit policy, the happier your customers will be.

You probably know your customers pretty well—and you should. If you don't, you could very well end up with a pile of unpaid invoices and no idea how to recover the money owed on them. Don't let this happen to you.

Credit policies are a must for every business that extends credit. Any company that doesn't accept payment at the time of the sale must have a policy in place or run the risk of losing money and sales. If this gets out of control, you can end up with many customers owing you and no money coming in.

ELEMENTS OF A CREDIT POLICY

There are five major elements to any credit policy:

1. Mission
2. Goals
3. Responsibility
4. Policies and procedures
5. Terms of sale

Your *mission* is a statement of what you want this policy to do for your business. For example, your mission might be that the credit department will offer credit to all customers that fill out an application and are found creditworthy.

Each company's *goals* will differ depending on the credit policy, and they should reflect your credit department's overall objectives. Your credit department's goals might be to operate with a certain number of collectors for a specific number of accounts, while also keeping bad debt down to less than 2 percent of all sales. You might want to consider establishing new goals annually and basing them on sales, competition, and/or the economy. You could then list those goals each year in your updated policy. An example: "All customers should be contacted by phone if they become 15 days past-due, and contacted by mail if they become 25 days past-due. Any past-due accounts not having had a payment posted to them in 3 months, and that are over 90 days, will be sent to a collection agency. All credit applications should be updated and rerun every 6 months."

Your *responsibility* should reflect the accountability or authority of your credit manager or whoever has been sanctioned to enforce your company's credit policy. For example, your credit manager would have final authority to check and either approve or deny customers' credit, credit limits, revoke credit, or put accounts on hold. This section would state the duties of all related personnel.

Your *policies and procedures* would list how everything will work within the credit function. This includes your payment terms, new account processes, credit applications, checking credit, pulling credit reports, setting credit limits, when and how to contact customers, making sales when a customer is past-due, disputes, bad debt, and using a third party collection agency as well as all other issues relating to the credit and collections function. An example of a policy might be that you will not grant a customer a line of credit unless they've completed and signed a credit application. Another could be that accounts can only be placed with a collection agency upon approval of the sales department or VP of Finance.

Finally, your *terms of sale* are your payment terms—including how and when you want to get paid, as well as the parameters you've listed on your credit applications, invoices, statements, and website. You would just list your terms, for example "net 30," and all other terms or discounts must be approved by the credit manager. There are six steps you need to take as part of your policy each time you have a potential new customer.

1. Completing the new account form
2. Completing the credit application

3. Checking credit
4. Setting credit limits
5. Notifying the customer
6. Updating credit limits

Though the new account form is not required, it can be an incredibly helpful way of gathering general information such as name, address, contact information, how the customer heard about the company, who they currently use for this service and what their experience with them has been, and why they want to change companies. Knowing what potential customers want and didn't get from another company lets you provide great service to them. By comparing customers' experiences with other companies, you gain an advantageous insight into customer satisfaction.

If you don't implement a credit policy or credit management plan, do make sure that you always get a signed credit application. This single document will help you in so many ways if you ever have a problem with the customer—for instance, if their phone becomes disconnected, their mail is returned, or you have to take them to court or place them with a collection agency or attorney. The application will have all the information a third party will need in order to investigate the customer, contact them at work, or locate them if they have skipped town. It also provides a Social Security number to help with credit reporting.

You can check credit in a few different ways. One is to become a member of one of the credit bureaus and pull credit reports. Or you can manually check credit by calling references, vendors, banks, and anyone listed on the credit application.

It's certainly tougher to set credit limits without a credit report, since you have to determine on your own what salary this person makes and what their expenses might be. You don't know if the customer has any credit cards, whether they are past-due, or even if they have been placed with a collection agency before.

It's also a good idea to recheck customers' credit once or twice a year. Similarly, if you read something in a trade journal or newspaper about a company having financial issues, you might want to review their account and reevaluate their credit limit. Keep in mind that if you do change the credit limit in either case, you must notify your customer and tell them why.

Below, you'll find an example of a credit policy that has each of the elements mentioned above. Take a close look at each component to see how they work together to form a cohesive plan.

CREDIT POLICY FOR ABC COMPANY
Mission

The Credit Department will offer credit to all customers that fill out and sign a credit application and are found to be creditworthy.

Goals

The Credit Department's goals are to operate with one collector per 700 accounts while keeping bad debt down to less than 2 percent of total sales.

All customers found to be 15 days past-due will be contacted by mail.

All customers found to be 20 days past-due will be contacted by phone.

Accounts over 90 days old with no payment activity in the previous three months will be placed with a collection agency that has been approved by the credit manager.

All credit applications will be updated and rerun every six months.

Responsibility

The Credit Manager has full authority over all aspects of the credit and collections functions.

The Credit Manager reports to the Chief Executive Officer.

Policies and Procedures

No customer will be given a line of credit without completing and signing a credit application.

Customers' terms cannot be changed without the Credit Manager's approval.

No accounts may be placed with a collection agency without the Credit Manager's approval.

Accounts looking for a credit limit higher than $5,000 must be approved by the Chief Executive Officer.

Terms of Sale

Two percent 10 days, net 30 days.

$25 fee on returned checks.

Court costs and collection fees can be added to balances placed with a collection agency or taken to court for payment.

All other special terms or discounts must be approved by the Credit Manager.

SKILLS AND RESOURCES NEEDED FOR
SUCCESSFUL CREDIT MANAGEMENT

You want to make sure your credit management plan covers these six areas:

1. How to apply for credit
2. Late fees, interest fees, collection, court, or bad check fees
3. Repayment terms and conditions
4. Credit limits
5. Buyer responsibilities
6. Seller liability

There are certain tools that are essential for a credit manager to effectively do his or her job. An absence of just one of the following tools can provide a crack through which a debtor may slip.

- Signed credit application
- Full knowledge of the FDCPA and additional state laws
- Communication skills
- Negotiation skills
- Skiptracing or location skills
- Mediation skills
- Organization skills
- Creativity
- Flexibility

There are a few areas in which you might consider getting professional training. Some of these are developing your telephone voice, refining your listening skills, managing the emotional side of debt collection, organization prior to making any calls, preparing your opening statement, and closing the call.

Normally, credit managers are responsible for managing all lines of credit, providing account and payment support service to customers, evaluating credit risk, assessing new customers' creditworthiness, and authorizing new revolving credit accounts. It is also their job to negotiate terms and conditions to minimize risk exposure, manage any customer disputes, keep customer records and credit applications, set credit limits, review credit performance of accounts, enforce a credit policy, and improve cash collections.

Clearly, credit managers must have strong communication and organizational skills, and be able to solve problems in a positive way.

Having been a first-party and a third-party bill collector—and having trained collectors for both positions—I know from experience that the most difficult aspect of being a collector is dealing with debtors either on the phone or in person. In my view, the most important part of collecting is following the laws—especially since they keep changing—keeping your cool, and staying in control of the situation so you can get paid. I've found that the best way to achieve this is to be educated. If you know the laws and prepare responses for debtors' potential excuses or comebacks, you will be able to answer the debtor no matter what the scenario and, even more important, offer a solution. One of the ways I approached this with the collectors that worked for me was to test them on the laws and have them listen to me make collection calls. I provided them with charts for their desk with common excuses and examples of replies. The more collection calls you make, the better you get at it and the more experience you will have dealing with common excuses and how you should respond.

FOLLOWING FEDERAL AND STATE LAWS

It is simply good business practice to know what laws are out there—even if they do not necessarily apply to you. One law that applies to third party collectors and attorneys who regularly collect debts for others (but does not apply to business owners collecting their own debts) is the Fair Debt Collection Practices Act. The FDCPA was created to protect consumers and became effective March 20, 1978. Being aware of the FDCPA provides you with structure and guidelines for your credit policy. If you learn and follow this law, you will see that you will have much more success collecting from your customers.

Another law, called The Fair Credit Reporting Act (FCRA), originally passed in 1970, was designed to promote accuracy and ensure the privacy of the information used in consumer credit reports. This law ensures that consumers have access to information about them that lenders, insurers, and others obtain from credit bureaus and use to make decisions about providing credit and other services. The FCRA also requires that users of credit reports (which would be you if you wanted to check credit through use of credit reports) have a "permissible purpose" to obtain them. It also mandates that credit reporting agencies maintain the security and integrity of consumer files, and allows consumers to limit certain uses of their reports. Your "permissible purpose" would be to extend credit—thus the importance of a signed credit application.

WHY SHOULD YOU HAVE A CREDIT MANAGEMENT PLAN?

There are so many reasons you need this. A credit management plan, for example, does the following things:

- Provides timely notification to your customers regarding any past-due amounts, therefore eliminating old balances from being carried as receivables.
- Outlines a procedure that will provide your customers with options when they cannot pay in full or on time.
- Establishes a procedure on when and what to do with small balances on customers' accounts.
- Enables you to adequately provide reasonable credit limits for customers with revolving credit accounts.
- Sets guidelines to legally collect money due to your company that was lost because of bad checks.
- Establishes a system that will maintain timely contact with your customers when their accounts are past-due. It also provides a procedure that enables your business to keep credit card numbers and checking account information on file for customers and automatically charge them when they place an order or for scheduled monthly or weekly payments.
- Makes your business aware of when an account should be placed for collection and thereby helps you avoid carrying bad debts on the receivables.

- Eliminates orders being held for nonpayment and will better service customers in a timely manner.
- Alerts you as to when to write off a balance to bad debt.

Having a credit management plan in place can help your business be successful, make more money, and more sales. Credit has traditionally been used to allow individuals to live beyond their means, or because some are not dedicated enough to save money for something that they want *now*. Many people have a cavalier attitude toward credit and seem to feel as though it is owed to them. Keep in mind as you work on your credit management plan that credit is a privilege that you as the business owner extend to customers you find worthy of it.

People apply for credit for all sorts of reasons. For some, credit fulfills self-esteem issues by enabling them to "buy" friends by picking up the check or paying for movie tickets when they don't really have the money. Some use credit for a feel-good activity such as shopping (the number-one feel better activity when someone is depressed or sad). Even the most educated people with very good jobs and big paychecks get so far into debt that they file for bankruptcy and fall into a depression. Credit problems are not "poor" or "rich" person problems; rather, they are a people problem that frequently stems from personal issues. Consider the following transformation in credit trends:

Then: People used to be ashamed to file for bankruptcy.
Now: Many people suffer from credit card dependency and there is no longer any shame in being in debt.

USING CREDIT MANAGEMENT TO IMPROVE COLLECTION PROCEDURES

I've written countless credit policies for a variety of businesses—large and small, retail and service—policies that have helped them all to make more money. People frequently ask me what my books can do for them—and who exactly needs these books. Some potential answers are:

- Anyone who wants to start their own business.
- Driven and ambitious people who like to see the results of their work.
- Business owners who have money owed to them.
- Business owners who do not have a credit policy for their business.
- Entrepreneurs who want to be their own boss and make their own future.

Using this book for your business will help you collect money from your customers in a fast and effective way. You'll be able to see the actual results of your work reflected in your bottom line. You will collect more money and be more successful. You will learn how to weed out and fire slow or nonpaying customers that are dragging you and your business down.

Now for the most popular question I am asked: "How do I create a credit policy and why do I need one?"

A credit policy is just as necessary to a company as a business plan or a marketing plan. Without a business plan, you won't be able to get a loan to start your company. If you don't have a marketing plan, you will not have the media exposure you need or a way to get the word out. And if you don't have a credit policy, you will not be in control of your cash flow or your company's success. Any credit policy you create should be included in your business plan, along with your marketing strategy. The bank that you approach for a loan will see that you have done your research and that you are very serious about your business, how it will be run, and how you will be making money to pay them back. Incorporating your credit policy in your business plan gives you a much better chance of being approved for a loan.

It's important to keep in mind that, just as every business or marketing plan is different, every credit policy is different as well. It is based on your goals for your company and how much money you want to make. Your credit policy has to reflect your customer service procedures, your product, and how you want your cash to flow. There are so many things to know when you create your policy, including the laws in your state and the states in which you will be doing business.

Some business owners have been running their companies for months or even years when they come to one of my talks about credit policies, limits, and applications. Inevitably, some will say to me, "I never did any of that and I have so many customers that owe me money and are past-due." Many think it is too late to do anything about it, or are afraid to ask a customer for the money or to fill out a credit application. But why worry about alienating a customer who is past-due or not paying you? This is a customer you do not need. Wouldn't you rather have a customer that pays you? Stop working for free.

If you have customers that owe you money right now, today, you can and should do something about it *immediately*.

I would bet that if you add up how much money is past-due or not being paid, the dollar amount will shock you. That alone should emphasize that *now* is the time to do something about it! The next section lists some actions every business owner can take today to start making more money by collecting what is owed to the business. Do not wait; after all, you're in business to make money, aren't you?

ACTION STEPS FOR YOU TO TAKE TODAY

1. Review your accounts receivable and find out who owes you money, how much, and how many days past-due it is. Print this list or put the invoices in a pile.
2. Set aside one hour each day to sit down and call those customers, or have someone in your office call them for you.
3. Create a series of collection letters to send out to the customers who are approaching the past-due mark or who are 30 to 60 days past-due and whom you could not reach on the phone. If you do not have any collection letters, check out one of mine, as well as forms from books for actual letters that I have used. They are very effective.
4. Mail those letters *today*.
5. Put a note in your calendar to call those people in one week if you do not have their payment. If you can't reach them by phone on that day, send another letter the same day.
6. Follow up on all phone calls and letters. If you don't do this, then don't bother to do anything, since following up is the most vital step you can take in collecting what's due to you.

You worked hard to have your own business and you deserve to get paid. Don't let your customers control your cash flow. Take the above steps and see an immediate increase in your collections.

Some other things you can do to gain knowledge or help you with collections are to network with other business owners who are doing the same thing. You can do so by joining my Credit & Collections Association and beginning to interact, exchange ideas, ask questions, and learn more about debt collection starting today. I am happy that my association is able to help entrepreneurs, credit managers, and collectors run their companies successfully and get every dollar they've earned.

Many people e-mail me questions about credit, debt collection, credit policies and procedures, and getting paid. The following is a list of the most frequent collection mistakes I've seen businesses make. In my 18 years as a bill collector, these stand out the most.

1. *Lack of a credit policy.* So many business owners do not bother to create a credit policy. They cannot expect to get paid if they don't outline how they want it to occur. This makes as little sense as making a deposit at a bank at which you don't have an account.
2. *Extending credit to anyone who walks through the door or calls to place an order.* I personally know of many business owners that do this. They are so excited to make a sale that they do not check credit, outline terms, or even get any information from the customer. Then when the person doesn't pay, or the check bounces, the creditor doesn't know what to do next. I've even met

business owners who extended credit to a new customer without even getting the customer's last name!

3. *Receiving "non-sufficient funds" or "bad" checks.* This is the most popular yet. I cannot stress this enough: Be prepared *before* you receive a bad check. Make a sign to hang in your store or post on your website or both that tells customers what you charge when a check is returned, and what will happen to the account if a check is returned. Avoid receiving bad checks in the future by having every customer fill out a credit application—and then *check their references!*

Business owners can charge an NSF or "bad check fee" when they receive a check back from their bank. However, business owners don't know how much that fee is, and it differs from state to state. You can check my Credit & Collections website or the Law Dog website for updated bad check fees.

And keep in mind that bad check laws do not apply when an individual stops payment on a check—unless it can be proven that the check's issuer intended to stop the check when he or she first presented it for payment. Some states authorize the receiver of that bad check (you) to collect a service charge to compensate for bank fees and/or the costs incurred as a result of receiving and collecting on a bad check.

COMMON CREDIT MANAGEMENT MISTAKES AND HOW TO CORRECT THEM

If you are creating your credit policy you may not be familiar with some common mistakes made when collecting on past-due accounts. Make sure you don't fall into any of these traps:

- Failing to check customers' credit history before extending credit.
- Not getting a signed credit application, agreement, or contract.
- Being unfamiliar with the FDCPA and unintentionally harassing a debtor.
- Overlooking small balances.
- Not asking for the money because it makes you uncomfortable.
- Failing to know when it's the right time to turn the account over to a collection agency.
- Failing to have—and/or enforce—any type of credit policy.
- Extending credit to anyone who walks in or calls because they "sound like they will pay."
- Not taking action on returned checks.
- Not using letters and forms to collect on past-due accounts.
- Not having a credit application and having customers fill it out.
- Not checking potential and current customers' credit.
- Not understanding how to communicate with customers to keep them current with payments.
- Not using discounts and incentives to persuade customers to pay early.
- Not knowing how to set up realistic payment schedules with customers.

- Not knowing what to do if a customer files for bankruptcy.
- Not training your collection staff properly.
- Waiting too long to use a collection agency.

Even if you've already made some of these mistakes, there are things you can do to correct them, such as taking the following steps:

- Enforce your credit policy. It's never too late for this, so start today.
- Make sure your debtors are worth something before suing them. If they don't have any assets, a job, or a bank account, there is nothing to attach or garnish if they do not pay.
- Ask for payment immediately when it is due.
- Research and sign up with a debt collection agency even before you need one and then place accounts before they get too old.

Always check credit references, and keep in mind that if something doesn't seem right, it's probably not. If you are not happy with the references provided to you, ask for additional ones. This customer wants credit from you, so *you* call the shots. If, on the other hand, you give them credit without checking them out, *they* call the shots.

Now that you have an idea about credit policies, be sure to periodically evaluate how your own credit policy is working for you and your business. It is up to you to be on top of this and to make sure you get paid for the work that you do. There are two easy things you can do to strengthen your credit policy right away.

1. Make sure you have a signed credit application with up-to-date contact information on file for every customer.
2. If you haven't satisfied number one, mail a new credit application to all of your credit customers along with a cover letter explaining that you are updating your files and need their current information.

Depending on how many accounts you have, number one might take you some time. If you don't have very many accounts, you will get the best results by calling the customers that owe you the most money first. Work your way down based on the total dollar amount owed. Send a collection letter with a payment envelope to anyone you don't have time to call. If you find that you just don't have the time during the week to do this, pick a night or a weekend day and make it a priority to get it done. You will be glad you did when the money starts coming in, which will motivate you to continue. If you just don't have time to do any of these things, you can still outsource this task to a collection agency. This works well because you don't pay anything if the collection agency doesn't collect anything.

Number two will help you because you'll now have a credit application for customers for whom you didn't before. You'll also have up-to-date information for customers with old applications, and will be able to reevaluate customers to make sure that their creditworthiness matches their credit limit.

I receive questions every day from business owners on a variety of collection and payment problems that they run into.

By sharing one here, I can give you an example of what other business owners are encountering and how they deal with those problems. The following story came from someone who owns and runs a locksmith company.

I run a mobile locksmith business in Colorado. Recently, a local used car dealership requested my services to make new keys for six of their repossessed vehicles. I provided them with the cost of the service in writing and had them initial this paperwork before I began the job. Once completed, I asked them what form of payment they would be using. They informed me that they cut checks on Fridays and would mail me the check. That was several weeks ago, and I have not yet received payment.

When I contacted the general manager about the late payment, he then informed me that he was not happy about the charges on my bill and would not send the payment until we renegotiated the price for my services. I informed him that he had agreed to the price before the job was done by initialing the bill/estimate and then signing the receipt—thereby promising payment—when the work was complete.

What can I legally do to expedite payment from this company? If I hire a collections attorney or agency, can I add the attorney or collection fees to the unpaid balance?

Unfortunately, the only way this man could add collection agency or attorney fees to the unpaid balance would be if he had provided for those fees on the paperwork signed by the customer *before* the job was done—and if the law in the state where the exchange occurred allows it. Another option would be to file with small claims court if the amount due is less than what is allowed; this way, the court will add any interest and fees. Once you have a judgment you can attach any assets.

My suggestion to him would be to begin the process by sending a final demand letter with delivery confirmation. He should include the letter, the copy of the signed paperwork, and any other paperwork such as the invoice or work order in a flat rate priority envelope. He must clearly state in the letter the specific date by which he must have payment in his hands. If he fails to receive the payment on that date, he should file with the courts.

It is also crucial that this business owner not accept another payment promise that can be broken once he sends the demand letter with a specific date—and to *not* back down from that date. If he accepts another payment promise and then doesn't get paid (again!), he'll lose all credibility. If he doesn't have his money by then, he must take action. He cannot waste any more time on the account, and should immediately process it through the small claims court process or a collection agency. He can avoid this problem in the future by getting a signed contract before ever doing any work for any customer. Every business owner needs to have contracts ready and available for each customer they work with. You can have a template ready and use the same one, or customize it for each customer. But without a contract, you won't have a leg to stand on when you want to be paid.

DEALING WITH BAD CHECKS

Accepting checks as a form of payment always comes with some element of risk. Some companies don't like to deal with bad or returned checks, so they simply refuse to accept them as a form of payment. That is one way to limit your credit risk in relation to checks, and is perfectly within your rights;

after all, accepting checks is a privilege you extend to your customers.

Here are a few other things you can do to avoid getting bad checks.

- Don't let the check writer rush you.
- Don't take any check or person for granted; *always* obtain proper ID.
- Don't accept pre-written personal checks; the signature should be written in your presence.
- Don't accept unsigned checks.
- Don't accept starter checks, which are the checks a bank gives you when you open a new checking account and your own checks have not arrived yet. Starter checks normally do not have anything imprinted on them such as a name, address, or even a check number.

If you do decide you will accept checks, make sure to:

- Check that the name, address, and phone number are imprinted on the check.
- Accept checks with the *current date* only.
- Compare the ID picture with that of the person cashing or writing the check.
- Make sure the check and ID signatures match.
- Make sure the phone number is a working phone.
- Ask for a physical or street address if only a P.O. box is listed.

Writing a bad check is a crime in every state, one punishable by a fine and/or imprisonment. Yet there are an estimated 450 million bad checks written every year. This includes checks written without sufficient funds or upon accounts that have been closed. Bad check laws do not apply when an individual stops payment on a check unless it can be proven that the check's issuer intended to stop the payment when he or she presented the check. Some states authorize the bad check's receiver to collect a service charge to compensate for bank fees and/or any costs incurred as a result of receiving and collecting on a bad check. Be sure to check your particular state's statutes for the current fees or laws on what you can add to a bad check balance legally.

TOP METHODS FOR IMPROVING COLLECTION PROCEDURES

Some businesses end up having slow paying customers or past-due balances because they didn't train their customers from the beginning. You must always let your customers know about your credit policy and/or terms of payment before they even become customers. Reiterating your credit policy when payment is overdue is a good step to take in trying to obtain payment. You should also never extend credit to a new customer without having them complete a credit application and undergo the credit approval policy. It is essential to maintain accurate records on an account payment history once you extend credit, and to follow your collection policies no matter what.

Change your collection letters frequently to make them stronger and more action-oriented.

Discourage payments on account or changes in payment terms, as too many of these can impair your cash flow. Be sure to follow up right away with a letter or phone call to thank customers for payment when you receive payments "on account." Let them know what their new balance is, and tell them—don't ask—when to send the next payment.

On large accounts, call or send a reminder just a few days after terms if they become past-due.

Ask to speak to a manager or owner when making collection calls rather than a secretary or receptionist. You want to go directly to the decision maker.

Update your records often, and make sure you have current and up-to-date telephone numbers and addresses for your customers. You can immediately improve your collections if you follow the four steps right away with the accounts that have largest past-due balances. Let's imagine the following scenario.

You called John Smith this morning for the 18th time and left another message; also, you have found out that John recently bought a new truck and is renovating his home. When you left a message this morning, you were told John is away on vacation. You haven't collected any money from John in months and your boss is chewing you out. Since your phone calls are obviously not working, you decide to write a "Dear John" letter. Follow these steps:

1. Make the letter brief and to the point; it's best to be blunt. For example: We need to receive your payment by Friday 11/12/2012 at 5:00 P.M. Another example could be: Since we have not received a payment or a response from you, your account will be placed with a collection agency on Friday 11/12/2012 unless we receive payment in full before that date.

2. Use a larger font in the important parts of your letter—such as the balance that is due, the action you may take, or your mailing address.
3. Give a payment deadline that includes day of the week, date, and time; state what will happen on that date if you don't receive payment.
4. Send this letter in a flat rate priority mail envelope with delivery confirmation.
5. Some people worry that a priority mail envelope is going to cost extra. However, you simply pick up the envelopes for free at the post office or order them online at www.USPS.com. The postage is less than sending something by certified mail and much more effective. All of my clients that have used this approach have had fantastic results—so give it a try!

Whenever you're attempting to collect more money, remember to:

- Be confident.
- Be prepared—if you don't know what you are talking about you will fail.
- Express urgency to the customer.
- Smile.
- Listen.
- Sit up straight in your chair.
- Do not fidget or squirm.
- Focus.
- Pay attention.
- Dress professionally.

- Present a call to action confidently and simply.
- Be ethical, courteous, and polite.
- Take notes and follow up.

You will collect more money if you have an understanding of credit and debt and how they affect your customers. To help you understand some of the things that can happen to a credit-approved customer to cause them to become past-due, I will use my own personal situation as an example. I had good credit until I got divorced. My credit went downhill as my divorce progressed. It was terrible to have bill collectors calling me and sending me letters, especially when I didn't have any money to pay them. Even though I had a full-time job, I had gone from having a two-person income to pay for my house, bills, and children down to a one-person income. Because I was the one who stayed in the home, I received all the calls. I was barely able to make my mortgage payment, pay my taxes, and then support myself and my children. Even more unfortunately, my ex-husband didn't feel the need to make child support payments; therefore, it was only *my* income that was available to me and my two young children. Since I was already working full time, I had to come up with a plan or I was not going to be able to stay in my house and care for my kids.

So I took out all of my bills and made a list of them. I then decided which bills I could eliminate in order to create more income for myself to pay my mortgage, and afford fuel for my car so I could continue to go to work and pay for utilities. Some of the things I eliminated or cancelled were cable television, my cell phone, all entertainment such as movies or going out, and unfortunately I had to find a new home for my dog. I then called the companies to which I owed money in order to explain my situation and see if there were any options. I called the electric company first, and they let me pay a small monthly amount until I could pay more. The phone company let me pay $10 to $20 a month toward my bill as long as I didn't make long distance calls or otherwise run up the bill. I then went to my town for assistance. Even though I was working full time, I had to go to my church for food—because I didn't have enough money to shop for groceries after paying my bills. Although it was admittedly pretty awful at the time, I am, in a way, fortunate since this experience helped me to be a better collector. I was able to understand where a past-due customer might be coming from, and was also able to offer advice on some tactics they could take to get out of a bad situation and pay their bills.

The following debt collection information will help you in creating your policies and procedures:

- Debtors cannot be put in jail because of failure to pay a debt.
- You can sue a debtor if they start making small monthly payments and you did not agree to accept them.
- Always record the date, time of day, name, and contact information of the person you call.
- Recording phone conversations without the consent of the other party is legal in some states.
- You cannot visit a debtor's home or call them before 8 A.M. or after 8:30 P.M.
- You cannot call a debtor at work if you know the employer does not allow this.

- You can contact other people to find debtors, but you cannot tell them it is because they owe money.
- If a debtor gives you an attorney's name, you can contact only the attorney.
- A debtor can stop you from calling by telling you not to call anymore.
- You cannot use threats of violence, profanity, any false statements, or repeated use of a telephone to annoy or harass or give false credit information about a debtor to anyone.

CREATING AN EFFECTIVE CREDIT POLICY

When the economy took a nosedive, business owners everywhere suddenly had to deal with making more collection calls than they had been used to in order to get paid. Foreclosures are now at a record high with no quick fix in sight, and home prices in ten major metropolitan areas in October 2010 were down 6.7 percent since 2009 at the same time. People are losing their jobs in many industries. All of this is making it more difficult for company owners to collect money. Credit flow through companies is drying up at a pace not seen in decades; in fact, you've likely noticed yourself that getting credit is becoming increasingly more difficult. It is crucial for your business to keep up-to-date on the foreclosures happening nationwide and in your area.

I hope that you already have a credit policy in place and won't have to scramble to keep your receivables under control as they grow— and the economy sinks. If not, however, there is still time to take steps to help you avoid this problem in the future and take care of it now. Take a look at your accounts receivable listing as well as your customers' credit limits, what they owe, how old the balances are, their payment history, and the last time their credit limit was reviewed. It's essential to determine how and to whom to extend credit; it's a step that should be updated at least once a year when setting credit limits. You should also be thinking about the criteria you have for any customer to whom you extend credit. You need to remember to limit your risk while building your business.

To determine how and to whom to extend credit, you need to gather information from your customers or potential customers—and the most painless way to do this is to use credit applications. These documents give you a wealth of information that you can use later if you are having trouble getting paid, such as:

- Contact information
- Credit references
- Bank references
- Employment information
- Financial information
- Permission to check references and/or pull a credit report

Before you start telling people about your credit policy, however, you need to know your billing procedures—so you can offer them credit based on how you want cash to flow through your business. This requires you to determine the following about your business:

- Your terms
- How and when you want to get paid
- How much risk you are willing to take

To determine how much credit to extend to a customer, ask yourself these questions:

- Do they have a pattern of paying some suppliers on time and others late?
- Is there chronic delinquency?
- Is there a seasonal pattern?
- Is any poor payment due to employment issues, a one-time event, or change in marital status?
- What are the customer's anticipated monthly purchases?
- Is cash okay until credit is approved?

And for customers who are businesses:

- Where is this company going?
- How long have they been in business?
- Who are their customers?
- What does the competition look like?
- Do they have any liens, bankruptcies, U.C.C. filings, or judgments against them?
- Have they ever been placed with a collection agency?

There are several things you can do to help protect yourself legally—as well as if you end up having to take any type of action to get paid—when you want to limit your risk while extending credit. You can get a personal guarantee, offer month-to-month credit, offer ship-to-ship credit, ask for a security deposit, and/or get a 50 percent deposit on every order.

I know that many people today are desperate for a quick fix. It may seem that many of your customers are suddenly losing their jobs or getting behind on payments. To that end,

I have listed six easy steps you can take today to help boost your credit policy and keep your customers on their toes.

1. Print out or buy credit applications (find one at www.michelledunn.com/free.html).
2. Put them on a clipboard at your front desk or door, or on your website.
3. Have every new customer fill one out.
4. Mail one to every existing customer, with a stamped addressed envelope.
5. Check all references.
6. E-mail me with any questions: michelle@michelledunn .com.

If you didn't have a credit policy before and simply printed out a sample to start taking these steps, congratulations—you have one now. Credit policies don't have to be difficult and confusing; they can be as simple as you want. However, not having one is always a recipe for disaster—something that many companies will be discovering in the current economic situation.

Your credit policy will be based on your terms, due dates, and what you want to happen when a customer is late or doesn't pay. Some questions to think about when you are setting your payment terms are: How often do you want to get paid? Do you want to be paid upon completion of the work, or would you like to offer 30-day terms? Maybe you want to offer 30-day terms with a discount if the invoice is paid in full within 10 or 15 days.

Some people really don't think about when they want to be paid. Consider the importance of this question, though—when will receiving that money benefit you and your company *the most*? It might be right before your bills are due so that you have the cash on hand to pay them on time. Maybe you even want to pay them early to take advantage of early pay discounts—thus saving yourself even more money. No matter what you decide upon for terms, choose a time of the month that you want to be paid—the first of each month, the 15th, or any date that works best for your business—and stick with it when setting your due dates.

Now, take a moment to picture yourself in the following scenario. You are sitting at your desk and a customer that you had great confidence would pay you is past-due and avoiding you. The balance is quite large, and the debt is getting older and older. What do you want to happen when your customer is late or doesn't pay you? Do you want their credit to be revoked? Their account to go on hold for future orders until this is paid? A phone call to be made or a letter to be sent?

Once you have a past-due customer or a bad check, you can take the following steps when customers are past-due, over their credit limit, or bouncing checks.

- Refer to your Credit Policy.
- Make a collection phone call.
- Send a friendly (or not so friendly) reminder.
- Revoke credit.
- Stay on top of your accounts receivables and follow up with anyone you contact.

If you are still having trouble with an account, go back to the sales department and talk to whoever made the sale. Sales will have gathered information on what the customer can and cannot afford; do not oversell! When an account is past-due, have the sales person who made the sale contact the customer.

The least popular method in getting the sales department to help collect is to withhold commissions on sales until customers have paid for the item in full.

It is absolutely vital for you to take these steps *before* your business is in a cash flow crisis. Make sure you have all of your credit-approved customers' accounts up-to-date and paid off in full. Take steps now to resolve any issues if anyone is past-due. Review all your credit-approved customers and make sure you have a current and up-to-date credit application, as well as a credit limit that works well for both them and you. Watch customers who may be in danger of losing their jobs or their homes, because chances are that they will not be able to pay you if this happens.

The following list of "Top 10 ways to avoid bad debt" is comprised of things you can start doing right now. Even if you just try one new thing a week, at least you are doing *something* that will help you maintain control of your cash flow.

1. Stay on top of balances owed.
2. Contact a customer immediately if they start to get overdue.
3. Do not continue to ship products to a customer who is not paying on time.
4. Reevaluate credit limits once a year.
5. Get a signed credit application from every customer.
6. Check references.
7. Stay firm!
8. Follow up.

9. Send invoices immediately after products are shipped or service is performed.
10. Fire customers who are not profitable.

According to psychologists, up to 90 percent of human behavior is habitual. If you have a habit of letting your receivables get overdue—a fairly common unsuccessful habit—you will always get a predictable result. Negative habits breed negative consequences, so you want to choose a better, more successful habit to replace this one. Three steps you can take to change this habit are to:

1. Review your accounts receivables weekly or, at the very least, monthly.
2. Stay motivated by trying to collect as much money as possible.
3. Stay focused; don't allow customer excuses to get you off track.

Once you have these habits in place, keeping your receivables up to date will be your new habit—one that will make you more money and grow your business.

The following is a recap of the best steps you can take to help you achieve success with your credit policies.

1. *Get more information than the P.O. box number.* To increase your collection agency's chances of tracking down an individual or business, always ask for the customer's physical address, phone number, and Social Security number. All of this information will be helpful in finding individuals, even if they have closed their P.O. box or changed their address and phone number. This

information helps the agency do a better job in collecting for you.

2. *Check credit and get a signed Credit Application.* Fend off collections problems from the very beginning by running credit checks on new clients and by discussing your prices, service fees, and payment requirements with new customers before you do any work for them. Carefully check credit references of each new account and don't extend more credit than the business can handle.

3. *Explain transaction terms thoroughly.* When extending credit, make sure that accounts know when you expect payment, and clearly detail any credits or penalties for early or late payment.

4. *Follow up overdue accounts.* Always be prompt when sending statements and reminders of payment due dates. Make phone calls if necessary.

5. *Institute a series of overdue notices.* Schedule regular written and oral reminders before you even consider using a collection agency.

6. *Set an absolute due date—and stick to it.* As a final step, establish a firm due date before you turn the account over to a collection agency. Do not extend this date, but do give the debtor warning of it. Once this date has passed with no payment, then you can place the account with a collection agency with the knowledge that your customer has been properly notified.

REMEMBER

Make your customer aware of the terms when you make the sale or at the time of the order. Customers are usually happy to comply if they see your stated credit terms right from the beginning.

Make your reminder friendly at first; many businesses pay 90 to 120 days after purchase. You can send a notice to speed up payment via e-mail or fax; both are effective ways to touch base with a slow paying customer.

Next, make a phone call. You should always assume payment has been made and ask "When did you send your check?" Then don't say anything. Let the customer break the silence no matter how long or uncomfortable it may seem.

Finally, pick up the payment in person. Once you show up in person to pick up a payment, you should never have to do this again—that is, if the customer has every intention of paying. If, however, you repeatedly have to visit their place of business, you may want to put them on a COD basis.

WHAT *NOT* TO DO

- Don't tell your friends at the monthly Chamber meeting that the customer is a deadbeat.
- Don't plaster online bulletin boards or mailing lists with notes telling the world that your customer is a bad credit risk.
- Don't hang copies of the bad checks around town or in your place of business.

Doing things like this can get you sued. You can also get yourself into legal hot water by making threats, using harassing or abusive language, making collection calls at odd hours or too often, or by making false statements about what will happen if the debtor doesn't pay. Creditors need to be aware of the FDCPA even though they are not required by law to follow it unless the state laws specify that they mirror or follow the FDCPA.

2

How Credit Affects Businesses

If you don't have a credit policy for your business, then everyone will want to do business with you! While this may sound appealing at first, you won't be doing yourself any favors. Extending credit to anyone and everyone without taking precautions, researching, and making sure a customer is creditworthy will leave you with a mountain of unpaid and past-due invoices on your books. Most new companies rely on their income more than veteran organizations because new businesses experience somewhat more sporadic income. New business owners are excited when they make a sale; they are finally getting paid for what they love to do! Or so they think. But what happens when you make that sale and then payment is not forthcoming? Now you are still doing what you love—but for free.

Remember—you always want to have a signed contract, agreement, and/or a signed credit application. If you're making a sale for a large amount of money, you might want to get half or a large portion of the payment up front and the balance upon completion of the job or delivery of the item. You can certainly set up special terms and have specific contracts and agreements for these types of large purchases. Common terms when offering financing for a larger purchase are one-half down at the time of the order and the balance at the time of completion. You can also break up the final payment into two, three, or even four smaller payments; it's certainly up to you. However, whatever you decide, you should always make sure that the person has some good credit; otherwise, they won't be making those final smaller payments.

HOW A BUSINESS CAN OBTAIN CREDIT

Starting a business is overwhelming enough in and of itself—never mind having to think about credit. But credit is an incredibly important part of the equation, since your company will need good credit to maintain its momentum and become more profitable. Fortunately, there are several ways to build and maintain good credit. For example, you might have to apply for a business loan to start your company; this will show up on your business credit report. Make sure if you do take out a loan that it's a payment that you can realistically and punctually make. Try to pay it off early (as long as there aren't any early pay penalties; ask your bank about this before signing any paperwork). Realize that this loan will be your most important payment each month and make it the first bill you pay (the next being rent).

You might also find yourself applying for credit with vendors or suppliers, which can also help you build up some credit to apply for a business credit card down the road. If you purchase supplies for your business—such as materials for the restroom, office supplies, shop equipment, or anything else—ask those vendors if you can apply for a charge account where you can order and receive a bill to pay. This will help you to build your business credit with them; you can then use them as a reference as long as you pay them on time. When you apply for a business credit card, you can list your business loan and these suppliers as references. Even a small line of credit can grow as your business grows.

If your suppliers offer you credit and send you an invoice, pay attention to see if they offer an early payment discount, and take advantage of it if they do. It not only helps your business credit; it will save you money.

THE IMPACT OF BAD CREDIT ON YOUR BUSINESS

It's best not to apply for credit when you start a company if you don't have the income to be able to pay it back; after all, no credit is better than bad credit. Bad credit will cause you to incur late fees, make it more difficult to obtain credit, and hurt your credibility. You then lose any discounts you might have been able to utilize as well as potential credit references. Though it is illegal to publish the names of people or businesses that don't pay, word still gets around within an industry.

If you cannot afford to buy on credit or don't have the references to apply for it, you should purchase your supplies from your vendors by prepaying or using COD for as long as you have to. Doing so will help you to create a credit history with that company, which will allow you to obtain credit from them. Once you have done this and you apply for credit, you will see how you can easily create credit for your business. However, it is much harder to correct bad credit once you have created it.

WHY YOU SHOULD EXTEND CREDIT AND HOW TO DO IT

Many businesses think they will play it safe and just get paid at the time of service; they figure that, this way, they don't have to put their company at risk by extending credit. However, extending credit works in your favor in many ways.

- It increases customer loyalty.
- Having credit applications for new customers to fill out shows them that you plan to be around for awhile and

that you are interested in your customers. They feel like getting credit with you is a privilege you are offering them.

- It shows customers that your business is financially stable and that you care and are serious about your money, success, clientele, and future.
- It increases your sales, and therefore your bottom line.
- Studies show that customers will purchase more if they can pay later.
- Being selective about the application process conveys the fact that you're not desperate; otherwise, you would extend credit to anyone who walked through your door.
- It allows you to expand your customer base.
- Customers who are happy with your terms will tell other people about you. Word-of-mouth advertising is the best and cheapest advertising there is. You can also offer incentives or discounts for referrals of other credit-approved customers.
- It shows you are interested in your customers and want to help them by offering sales and discounts and a credit limit so they can buy more now and pay later.

BILLING AND PAYMENT TERMS

Of course, you want to know when you will be paid when you make a sale. Controlling the timing of payment is a huge determinant as to whether your business will survive or fail. To that end, it's essential to outline how and when you want to be paid if you extend credit to any new or existing customers. Be as specific as possible in regards to each factor, and let customers know—in no uncertain terms—what will happen if they do not meet those payment requirements. Remember: if you don't set the payment terms for your business, your customers will, and you probably won't be happy with those terms. You establish these parameters to protect your rights, limit your liabilities, and provide you with the security of getting paid for the goods or services you provide.

In addition to detailing how and when you want to be paid, your terms should clarify what circumstances will follow if payments are not made as agreed. Print out and take a good look at your accounts receivables aging report weekly or biweekly to determine whether your customers are becoming slower in their payments. If so, follow up with those customers now and get them back on track, maybe with a payment plan if they cannot pay in full at this time.

There are a few things you can do to improve your cash flow and help your customers pay your invoices on time.

- Offer discounts.
- Get 50 percent down at the time of the order.
- Check each customer's credit thoroughly.
- Sell old, outdated inventory at lower sale prices.
- Issue invoices immediately.
- Follow up right away with slow paying customers.
- Use a different color paper to print your invoices than your statements.
- Use a larger font on the total amount due and underline it twice.
- Have a call to action on your invoices in a large font, in a bright color—something such as PAY NOW or PAY IMMEDIATELY in red, blue, or green ink.

- Include postage-paid or pre-addressed payment envelopes with invoices or statements.
- Stamp or print an important message on the outside of the envelope you mail your bills in; you can use a rubber stamp or your printer. Some examples are:
  - Dated Material
  - As Requested
  - Confidential
  - Do Not Bend
  - Handle with Care
  - Personal

A few other questions to ask yourself when you are setting your payment terms are:

- How often do you want to get paid?
- Do you want to offer terms? If so, how long? 30 days? 45 days? 15 days?
- Do you want to offer discounts?

Setting up your billing and invoicing is as important as setting up your credit policy. These procedures will dictate how and when you get paid and what happens when you aren't paid. There is software available that allows you to e-mail the invoices to your customers; another option is to print them out and mail them. Using e-mail has become the method by which many businesses send out their invoices for the speediest payment. While it's certainly quicker than the postal service, it can still get lost in the mail. This approach can be helpful because if someone claims that they did not receive an invoice, you can e-mail it again while you are on the phone with them. Make sure you are not on their "spam" list so that your e-mail isn't blocked.

You should also set up your billing to be done at the time of each sale rather than once a month. Present your customer with an invoice immediately when you complete the work you've done—either in person, by mail, via fax, or e-mail. You will want to send out monthly statements that show all of your customers' activity, payments, and new charges, with an aging of their balance due. Include any information about offering online payment on your invoices and statements. The easier you can make it for a customer to pay, the better your chances are of getting paid, and on time.

According to Javelin Strategy & Research (a company that provides quantitative and qualitative research focused on the global financial services industry), consumers paid $88.9 billion dollars online with a credit card, $57.2 billion with debit cards, and $32.6 billion in other ways, such as checks, cash, money orders, or PayPal in the past year. It's especially important knowing these facts in order to make sure your business accepts the most popular forms of payment and increase your chances of getting the money owed to you.

INVOICING

Something to keep in mind is that if you do not set terms for your business, the law sets a default period of net 30 days. Of course, it is preferable to establish your own payment terms. You will want to include these on as many documents and places as possible—your invoices, statements, contracts, agreements, website, and credit applications. Some companies even print it on the back of their paperwork while others have it in small type along the bottom. This prompts your customer to agree to and acknowledge your terms of service and payment. This is also the time for you to change the terms and make a note of the new terms in their file or on their account if you are giving a special discount or extending the due date.

The following items are examples of payment terms. (Remember: If you do negotiate terms, the law allows you to challenge customers who try to impose terms and/or conditions upon you that remove your rights to claim late payment interest or compensation.)

- Payment terms are net 30 days from date of invoice. Seller reserves the right to require alternative payment terms, including, without limitation, a letter of credit or payment in advance.
- If payment is not received by the due date, a late charge will be added at the rate of 1.5 percent per month, 18 percent per year, or the maximum legal rate, whichever is less, to unpaid invoices from the due date thereof.
- All payments (checks) should be sent to: (Insert your address).
- All payments by wire transfer should be submitted to: (Insert your bank name, address, and contact person).
- If a buyer is delinquent in paying any amount owed to seller by more than 10 days, then without limiting any other rights and remedies available to seller under the law, in equity, or under the contract, seller may suspend production, shipment, and/or deliveries of any or all products purchased by buyer, or by notice to buyer, treat

such delinquency as a repudiation by buyer of the portion of the contract not then fully performed, whereupon seller may cancel all further deliveries and any amounts unpaid hereunder shall immediately become due and payable. If seller retains a collection agency and/or attorney to collect overdue amounts, all collection costs, including attorney's fees and any court costs, shall be payable by the buyer. The buyer hereby represents to seller that buyer is now solvent and agrees that each acceptance of delivery of the products sold hereunder shall constitute reaffirmation of this representation at such time.

- Include a line after the above statement for a signature and date on your new account forms and credit applications.

Always make sure your invoices and statements include the following:

- Your mailing address, URL, e-mail address, and toll-free number if you have one.
- Your price, any discounts, final or total amount due.
- Delivery specifications or directions; always include a phone number.
- Your payment terms.
- Your discount program in detail (as you will see next).
- Any late fee or interest program policies (as you will see next).
- Notice that you will seek compensation for any debt-recovery costs if not paid according to your terms and conditions.

LATE FEES AND INTEREST

If you decide to charge late fees or interest on accounts, make sure you include any information about them in your original terms and conditions that are printed on your paperwork for the customer. You cannot add them on to a balance once the account is past-due unless you have notified the customer about them *before* the sale. A late fee may also be called a monthly finance charge; so in order to charge this fee, you of course must figure out what your monthly finance charge is. You can do this by dividing the annual interest rate you want to charge as a late fee by 12 to determine your monthly interest rate. Next, multiply this monthly interest rate by the amount due to determine the amount of the monthly late fee. Check with your state to find out the maximum amount you can charge for a late fee and then decide what you want to charge. Be sure to research your competition to see what they are charging.

DISCOUNTS

No matter how small or new your business is, you can give discounts. Always show a total price and then the discount amount with the new price listed last. Some businesses will also add a line item that says something similar to, "You have saved $125.00." This may be a good idea if the discount is substantial. When the discount is small, I recommend that you leave the total off and list the percentage, such as 5 percent or whatever the discount is.

3

EFFECTIVE
PAYMENT
ARRANGEMENTS

OBJECTIVES OF PAYMENT ARRANGEMENTS

The reason to make payment arrangements is to improve your cash flow while helping your customers. You want to effectively outline policies and procedures that will help provide your customers with options when they cannot pay in full. After all, getting paid *something* is better than not being paid at all.

The more options for payment that you offer, the better your chances are of making a sale and getting paid promptly. For example, you might miss out on a lot of good sales opportunities if you only do business on a cash basis. There are many different options available for you to use. Some common forms of payment are:

- Credit cards
- Debit cards
- Personal and business checks
- Wire transfer
- Online payments
- Money orders
- Cash

Customers who are struggling financially will look at their bills and decide which ones they can afford to pay that month based on what is most important to them. Mortgage payments normally come first on that list, followed by things like food, phone, electricity, fuel, and daycare. However, it's your job to make your invoice important to them and to offer them realistic options so that they will be able to pay you each month.

HOW PAYMENT ARRANGEMENTS AFFECT YOUR BUSINESS

Many business owners don't like to offer payment plans because it means more bookkeeping for them and a hassle they don't want to manage. But there's something important to keep in mind in this scenario: Someone who owes you money and is struggling to pay the balance in full probably owes others money as well. Therefore, whoever takes positive action first or offers them a solution will get paid first. When you are able to work with your customers and set up a realistic payment plan you will:

- Increase profits and revenues
- Retain customers
- Improve your operational efficiency
- Increase your bottom line
- Minimize your risk
- Have less bad debt
- Be able to efficiently handle and control your accounts receivables

You can start by identifying which accounts need payment arrangements and contacting those customers before they become overdue. Discerning and working with these customers will maximize your cash flow and will dramatically affect your company's bottom line.

Payment arrangements will affect your business by providing you with some cash flow where you may not have had any. By offering these measures, you are extending a helping hand to your customers and your community while enabling your company to continue to stay in business and become more successful. If you do not offer payment arrangements, you risk having much lower cash flow, losing customers, and therefore becoming unable to pay your own bills. At worst, this can result in going out of business or filing for bankruptcy.

Offering payment plans lets your customers budget a set amount to pay to you each month, which will help them when money is tight. They'll know the exact amount they owe you, which is easier for them to handle than maybe making the entire payment. You'll still get paid, but it will be over time instead of a lump sum. This can also benefit your business because instead of not getting any of the money, you get a bit each month and can use that towards paying your own business bills.

ELEMENTS THAT AFFECT PAYMENT ARRANGEMENTS

Every day entrepreneurs struggle to stay in business, steer clear of bankruptcy, and avoid closing their doors. Some aspects of business that may not have been getting the attention needed in the past are now under scrutiny. If your company is struggling, it is imperative to your success to change in one way or another. Offering payment arrangements is more important now than ever before. Many organizations simply don't bother to think about their business credit or credit policies when the economy is booming. But as the economy falters, owners and consumers begin to encounter problems that they haven't faced before, and they don't always know how to handle them. For example, many companies are discovering that customers who have always been able to pay on time are having trouble paying their bills and staying current, and others who may have been slow payers are falling even further behind or are unable to pay at all.

You need to create positive steps you can utilize to keep your existing customers, get paid, and stay in business. Some of these tools are tactics we've already discussed such as offering payment arrangements. These procedures and actions must be outlined clearly so that you know what to do immediately when someone has a problem paying and you can take steps to help both the customer and yourself.

If customers are not working, they may have other sources of income to pay off bills. They may have credit cards that they can use to tide them over until they get a job, or maybe they are receiving unemployment benefits. You can also suggest a reputable credit counseling service for help.

WHEN TO SET UP PAYMENT ARRANGEMENTS

Take a look at your customers' accounts, what and how much they owe, how old the debt is, their payment history, and the last time their credit limit was reviewed. Once you have this information, you will notice which customers might need to set up payment arrangements. Some signs to keep an eye out for are larger balances due than in the past, taking longer to pay than they have in the past, or whether they've stopped ordering from you. If you notice any of these things, now is the time to set up payment arrangements with those customers.

You should also consider setting up payment arrangements when you find yourself unable to pay your own bills on time, or if you find that your daily deposits are much smaller than they have been. You can also do so if you realize that your customers are not paying like they have in the past. It is important to stay on top of these things and start offering payment plans before any of these things becomes a bigger problem. Nipping cash flow issues in the bud is a very important part of payment plans.

HOW TO SET UP PAYMENT ARRANGEMENTS

You only need to set up payment arrangements if a customer cannot make payment in full. You must always do this by talking with the customer, and then you must follow up by sending a written notice or letter reiterating what the arrangement is. The only way to make this work is to be very specific. The first line of your letter should say something similar to, "As per our conversation today (date)." Then you can go into detail on the terms to which you agreed, the total due, the number of payments, and the due date and amount of each payment. I cannot stress enough that you need to be very specific and detail oriented. It's even better if you can include a payment envelope.

Never start a call with a customer by asking how much they can pay; this will just set you up for failure. You must let the customer know how much you can accept in order to remain in control of the call—not the other way around. Once you ask the debtor how much they can pay, you lose all negotiation ability as well as control of both the call and the situation.

It is essential to communicate confidence when you are speaking to past-due customers, and remain relaxed, self-assured, and prepared. Remember, everything you do represents your company: how you speak, collect money, send invoices, and handle delicate situations. Some things to consider when speaking to customers and making payment arrangements are:

- *First impression*: When your customers realize you are calling about a past-due invoice, they may not be happy. You must portray confidence and smile when you speak into the phone; it will be noticeable in your voice.
- *Your voice* should be loud enough to be heard and sound confident – not so loud that it seems like you're yelling, but not too soft. You want your customer to hear you and understand everything you are saying.
- *Maintain eye contact* by staying focused on the call. Don't check your e-mail or watch the other people in your office; stay focused on the task at hand.
- *Relax!* Sit up straight, don't play with paperclips or pens, use your face, voice, and posture to send your confidence over the phone. Imagine the person is sitting across from you.

If you put these techniques into use, you will collect more money and have better results from the calls you make. Take steps to ensure you make your calls as effectively as possible the first time around, so that you don't have to get in touch with people repeatedly, thereby showing them that you're letting them control the situation.

When you're setting up each customer with their specific payment plans, decide how many monthly payments you can extend to the customer, and then divide the total amount due by the number of months you want the balance to be paid in. This will be the monthly payment. Make sure that you put the payment arrangement with any customer in writing. Let the customer know that if they cannot make a payment they must call you and let you know; they can't just skip the payment because this could void the agreement. This will keep the lines of communication open while helping your customers stay on track and keeping some cash flow through your business.

WHY TO OFFER PAYMENT ARRANGEMENTS

The most important reason to offer payment arrangements is, not surprisingly, to get paid. If a customer is avoiding you or becoming more delinquent, it is likely they just cannot pay the entire bill and don't realize they have the opportunity to set up a payment plan. In my years of doing collection work, many of the debtors I would call did not pay because they thought they had to pay the whole amount due. Once they realized they could set up a payment plan, they were relieved and able to start making payments. The key to offering payment arrangements and actually getting those payments is to be realistic.

If you treat your customers well, they will continue to be your customer even after their financial crisis is over. They will appreciate that you worked with them and will continue to be loyal and tell others about your business.

DECIDING WHO NEEDS A PAYMENT PLAN

Many business owners don't set precedence on payment plans. They merely accept whatever their customers offer as payment without any negotiation, which is a huge mistake that can cost them the customer, money, and business. Business owners need to maximize their in-house receivables, and they cannot get a handle on these without assessing the situation and negotiating a payment plan that works for them and the customer, and which is also beneficial to all involved.

You have to make payment arrangements that are both worth your while and feasible for the customer. If you set up a blanket payment arrangement for all of your customers at $100 a month, regardless of their balances, order history, or credit history, you will not get paid and your payment arrangements will fail. However, if you work with each customer to assess their specific situation and agree on a certain amount and schedule that the customer can realistically achieve, then you will get paid.

The following will help you recognize when customers may need payment plans.

- Keep an eye on your accounts receivables and credit limits.
- Send your invoice upon completion of the work or delivery. Do not wait!
- Offer more ways to pay—check, credit or debit card, online payment options.
- Make collection calls and set up any payment plans with someone who has authority, not an assistant or clerk.
- Be persistent and follow up.
- Hold orders until past-due balance have been paid.
- Communicate via as many channels as possible.

Of course, every case and situation is different. If, for example, you have a customer who suddenly comes into a lump sum of money, you may want to offer a settlement amount rather than a payment arrangement. This allows your customer to pay off the debt for a lesser amount but in one lump sum, and you get a bigger payment all at once. You will have to decide if you can afford to write off any portion of the debt – such as late fees, interest, or shipping charges – then offer the customer a lump sum settlement payment and give it a due date. Then if they aren't able to pay by the specific date, the offer is void. I have done this with great success; a good time to make the offer is when people get their tax returns, Christmas club checks, or a severance package from work. If they can't afford a settlement payment, go back to setting up a payment plan. But be sure you explain to them that the plan is for the entire amount due; they only get the settlement amount if they can make that payment in full by a specific date. And of course, as with any payment plan or settlement offer—put it in writing!

Specific steps for successful payment arrangements are:

1. Ask for payment in full.
2. If the customer cannot pay in full, offer to split the balance into two payments with specific due dates.
3. Gather information on the customer's financial status.
4. Ask open-ended questions that allow you to evaluate the situation.
5. Suggest weekly or bi-monthly payments, as opposed to the common monthly payments. This will give you more money per month and allow the debt to be paid off more quickly.
6. Come to an agreement that is beneficial and realistic for you and your customer.

7. Get a commitment and document it.
8. Send the customer a letter reiterating your understanding of the agreement.
9. Ask for a signature on that agreement.

Always start off by asking for payment in full; then, go down from there. Always aim high, such as first asking for 100 percent, then 80 percent, then 75 percent, and so on. If you leave it up to the customer, they are likely to offer the lowest possible amount, which probably won't help your situation at all, and it certainly won't help them. Try to get as much as you can as frequently as you can. Remember to:

- Send a confirmation letter the *day you make the payment agreement* with your customer.
- Send a payment reminder *10 days before* the payment is due.
- If you do not have the payment on the due date, send a letter informing the customer that they have *five days to pay* before the arrangement is revoked and they go back to full collection efforts on the full amount.

Another scenario: Let's say that you get the business owner or debtor on the phone. First, identify yourself and your company and state your reason for calling. If the person tells you they cannot pay anything, listen, and then ask specific questions to help you offer a solution. Some questions for a customer might be:

- Do you have a job?
- Does your spouse have a job?

- Are you collecting unemployment?
- When do you get paid?

For a business debt you can ask:

- How are your sales?
- Are you waiting to be paid by your customers?
- Are you actively trying to collect from those customers?
- What payment promises do you have?

Something else to consider with another business: Could you possibly start a barter relationship with this customer? If they offer a service or something else you could use in your business, think about making a barter arrangement to clear up the past-due balance. But whatever the case, learn as much as you can about your customer's financial situation and other bills so you can offer a realistic payment plan. If your payment plan is not realistic, it will not happen. Offer to reevaluate their payment arrangement if their financial situation changes.

SKILLS AND RESOURCES NEEDED FOR SETTING UP REALISTIC PAYMENT PLANS

Negotiation is a key skill that anyone who is trying to collect money needs to develop. Even if you agreed upon an amount at the time of the sale, you may have to negotiate later if payment is not made. The following are some of the skills you will need in order to be an effective negotiator.

Understanding the Negotiation Process

Highly effective collectors recognize that negotiations are indeed a *process*—one that requires an understanding of billing, credit approval, and payment procedures.

Focusing on a Win-Win Situation

This means that both parties feel like they have won during the negotiation and collection process. Good bill collectors help their customers try to solve problems and look for opportunities to make that possible. They also know when to be firm and limit what they do in order to reach an agreement that is beneficial to both parties.

Patience

Too many collectors try to go for the quick fix so they can get paid and move on to the next account. But good bill collectors know that patience is a virtue and that rushing the collection process only leads to a failure to obtain money. Always gather the necessary information *before* you contact your customer; then carefully consider possible solutions. This is critical because major mistakes can be made when you rush.

Confidence

Good collectors are confident when making a call or writing a letter. They aren't arrogant, rude, or cocky; they are confident and helpful. You must believe in your ability to reach a win-win agreement with the customer; this is something you obtain through experience.

Listening Skills

People will tell you just about everything you need to know if you ask the right questions or keep quiet long enough for them to continue speaking. The biggest mistake a bill collector can make is not listening, or even worse, interrupting a customer. If you simply stop talking for long enough and listen, you'll receive key information from your customer that will help you in your collection effort. When you call a customer and state the reason for your call or ask a question, *wait for the answer*, no matter how long the pause may be. The customer should always be the one to break that silence.

There are some other skills that will help you to work with your customers, including:

Managing the Emotional Side

Chances are that customers will get upset that you are calling them. They feel as though there are better and bigger things going on in their life other than your bill. They will cry, yell at you, swear at you, and hang up on you. When a customer does any of these things or launches into a long story about what has been happening in his or her life, you need to have some compassion, listen to the tale of woe, and then offer a solution that will get your invoice paid. This is when you could offer a payment plan or a different payment option.

Prepare a Pre-Call Plan

Before you ever pick up the phone to call a customer, do some research on the customer and their account. Make sure you know the invoice number, due date, total amount due and past-due, how past-due it is, the payment history, details of the order, and whether there were any disputed items before you even dial. When the customer asks you any question, you need to have an answer immediately; otherwise you lose time, money, and your footing on the call.

Have an Opening Statement Ready

This should be brief and to the point. You need to identify yourself and your company, tell the customer why you are calling, and let them know what you want. For example:

"Hi, this is Michelle from KTM Auto calling about your past-due balance of $500 on invoice #1234 dated 4/1/10. I am calling today to take your payment over the phone so that we can clear this balance from our account. Would you like to pay with a credit or debit card or by check?"

Then, *STOP. WAIT* for an answer, and always assume the debtor will pay. This is the point where they may tell you they can't pay in full. Then you can proceed to establish some kind of payment plan.

Always ask questions. Do so with precision to make the transition to the payment arrangement. All your questions should be clear and to the point; and of course, remain silent after each to give the customer a chance to answer. Make sure you *LISTEN*.

For example:

Customer: I can't pay; I don't have any money.
You: Are you working?

Customer: Yes, but I just started back to work and don't get paid for two weeks.

You: When will you be getting paid?

Customer: Next Friday, the 15th.

You: Okay, we can accept a payment of half the balance (give dollar amount) on Saturday, the 16th.

This might go on and on for a bit. The customer may tell you that they cannot pay half, and you will work down from there until you reach a realistic agreement. You can then send out your confirmation letter with all the details of the agreement. Make sure you call on Friday the 15th to remind them about making that payment.

For example:

"Hi, this is Michelle from KTM Auto calling to confirm you will be mailing your check for $50 tomorrow, Saturday the 16th, as we agreed."

When you are setting up payment arrangements with past-due customers, you have to remember that it helps to be interested in people and have good verbal and written communication skills. You want to be persuasive and persistent but with a level of sensitivity to deal fairly with people who might have found themselves in difficult situations. You must be able to stay calm under pressure, adapt to tricky situations, and have strong negotiation skills and the ability to explain monetary matters firmly and clearly. You should have some mathematical aptitude as well, which will help you explain financial terms, credit services and policies, and how payments work. It would do you some good as well to understand relevant legislation concerning data protection and harassment, and have office and computer skills.

ELEMENTS OF A PAYMENT PLAN

The following is an outline of the elements that comprise a realistic and successful payment plan. You can use this to set up your own effective payment strategy.

- Make contact with the customer.
- Ask for payment in full; the customer then lets you know that is not possible and asks for a payment plan.
- You ask the debtor some basic questions regarding their finances.
- Are you working?
- Is your spouse/significant other/roommate working?
- When do you get paid?
- What other debts do you have? (Credit cards, car payments, insurance, day care)
- Are you receiving unemployment?
- How are you paying your bills now?
- What is your profession or skills?
- If you are working, how much do you take home each week?
- These questions will help you to determine the approximate disposable income of the customer.
- Depending on the amount of income the customer has and the amount owed, realistically approximate what you can ask for in terms of monthly, weekly, or bi-weekly payments.
- Offer more than one option to the customer so they have a role in this decision.

WHY SHOULD YOU OFFER PAYMENT PLANS?

Establishing payment arrangements is a two-way street; you create the rules and your customers have to play by them if they want to do business with you. It is up to you to be fair, reasonable, and not intimidating.

You want to offer payment plans to keep cash flowing through your business. If you have customers that can't realistically pay in full and you don't offer a payment arrangement, you may not get paid. Offering payment options will get you your money, though the process may take place over a given amount of time.

TRACKING PAYMENT PLANS

Once you make a payment plan agreement with a customer, you need to track it or keep up to date on it by checking that the payments are coming in as agreed and following up when they are not. Let the customer know when you set up any payment plan that missing one payment means that they'll be asked to pay the balance in full. You may want to send letters with payment envelopes a few days before each payment is due; then follow up immediately if a payment is missed. Always make an effort to get a customer back on track before taking further action.

Utilize statements in your tracking process. This is fairly simple since most billing software offers the printing of statements as an option. Send out monthly statements to all of your customers, especially those with payment arrangements. This will show them the original balance due, what payments were made and the dates, and what the final balance is now.

THE GUIDE TO GETTING PAID

I always sent out monthly statements when I worked as a credit manager. I would print them all out and sort them based on how many days past-due a balance was. For example, I made a pile of the over 120 days, over 90 days, over 60 days, and over 30 days. I would send out the most past-due statements first, sometimes stamping them with a red stamp that said FINAL NOTICE or PAST DUE. The 60-day pile might get a stamp or a past-due sticker so that it would stand out. This might not seem like much—and perhaps even more work than it is worth – but these small steps really helped to get those balances paid quicker.

MISSED PAYMENTS AND HOW TO CORRECT THEM

Call a customer immediately if they've been set up on a payment plan and miss a payment. Let them know you need the payment right then or the account will go back to the collection department and further action may be taken. This might be reporting the debt to a credit bureau, putting their account on hold, revoking their credit, placing them with a collection agency, or even taking them to small claims court. Remember that whatever you tell the customer you "might" do is something you *must* do if they fail to pay. Otherwise, you will lose your credibility and all chances of getting paid. You would have sent them something in writing outlining the payments and letting them know what would happen if they missed a payment when you established the original payment plan.

TOP METHODS FOR IMPROVING PAYMENT PLANS

Letting your customer know you care about their account and their situation enough to work with them to help them get their bill paid is one of the most effective ways to improve your plans and collections process. Another valuable method is to offer the customer something that they perceive as special treatment. For example, you might offer to write off some of the interest or a late fee, or maybe you can offer to lower their interest rate for three to six months. This gives them some confidence that, as they pay the past-due amount, the balance is actually going down and not up because of fees. Another idea might be offering to void the final payment if they make all other payments on time.

Offering incentives has a huge impact on how quickly and willingly customers pay you. You may be able to help them out by, for example, suspending all collection calls or activity on the account during the time of the payment plan. Present them with various ways to pay, such as money orders, Western Union, checks, credit and debit cards, online payment options, or in person. You can also get checks up front or obtain authorization to charge a credit or debit card for a certain amount on a specified date each month or week.

To recap:

- Work *with* the customer.
- Offer special treatment and incentives.
- Suspend collection activity as they make payments.
- Offer a variety of payment options.
- Get authorization to charge credit or checking accounts each month or week.

FOLLOWING UP

If you do everything you just learned about setting up payment arrangements but skip this incredibly crucial step, you

THE GUIDE TO GETTING PAID

may not get paid. Following up with the customers to whom you grant special payment arrangements is critical to a company's profitability. While most customers are very agreeable when you are setting up a payment plan on the phone, they tend to forget all about it once they hang up. This is why it is imperative that you send the agreement in writing immediately after speaking to them, and monitor their account to make sure they are making the payments as agreed.

Though this sounds a lot like babysitting, you may not get paid at all if you don't do it. Stay on top of your payment plan accounts by printing out aging reports weekly or setting up a tickler file so you know when to contact a customer who is not making their payments as agreed. And follow through with any warnings you made to your customer regarding voiding the agreement if they miss a payment. Otherwise, you will never have any credibility or leverage with that customer again.

Sending a follow-up letter after each payment is a good idea as well, even if you send statements. Start the letter by saying "Thank you for your payment of $25. Your new balance is $150 and your next payment of $25 is due on Friday, May 1, 2011. I have enclosed a payment envelope for this upcoming payment."

Staying on top of it will increase your chances for success. This may seem like a lot of work on your part, but if you don't put the effort in, your customer won't—and you will not get paid.

PAYMENT ARRANGEMENT CHECKLIST

How much does the customer owe?
How old is the debt?

Have they ever been past-due or late before?

Do they have a job or income?

Review their credit limits and worthiness to adjust their credit limit.

What other bills do they have?

Can they split the balance into three payments? If not, increase the number of payments from three to five, six, and so on.

Can they pay weekly or bi-weekly? (This is better than monthly.)

Can you get the first payment now over the phone?

How can they pay—check, credit, debit card, online?

Set up a specific date for when the first and subsequent payments are due.

Let customers know that if they miss a payment or are late, this arrangement will be void and the entire balance will be due immediately.

Send a confirmation letter of your agreement along with a payment envelope.

Call the day before the next payment is due to make sure they will be mailing it on time.

Call the third day after the due date if you have not received the payment.

If they stop paying or stop communicating with you, revoke their credit and send them a demand letter for the full balance.

If they do not respond to the demand letter, report the debt to the credit bureaus, place them with an outside collection agency, or pursue through small claims court.

4

HANDLING
CUSTOMER
DEDUCTIONS

You now have a credit-approved customer who has been doing business with you for a couple of months. They have been paying on time and placing steady orders. Suddenly you receive a check with a deduction on it. It might just be a negative number listed on the check stub, or maybe the check is just for a bit less with no explanation. Whatever the case, deductions can impair your cash flow and take up valuable time, so you want to always address them right away. The more time you let go by before handling this issue, the harder it will be to get paid back if it is not legitimate.

When you receive a payment with a deduction, research it immediately. If you need to provide paperwork to the customer regarding the deduction, call them and tell them it is coming, and ask if they need any other specific documentation that you can include. Send the paperwork via certified mail with a signature, or use a flat rate priority mail envelope. When you receive notification that they have the documents, call them right away to find out the status. Do not get caught up in the game of sending the documentation two or three times; this is a stalling tactic. Stay on top of the situation and resolve it as quickly as possible. You also can fax or e-mail the documents for quicker resolution. Make sure the customer sends the payment immediately; do not allow another 30 days or any more time to pass.

If you have a customer who takes frequent deductions, you will want to note this on their account and maybe reevaluate your credit terms with them. You can incorporate something into your credit policy in regard to deductions and make sure your customers are aware of this policy. For example, you might want to ask that all deductions be approved, and require that they have accompanying documentation to support them when they are deducted from a payment. This way, if these things don't happen, or you have a customer more than 120 days past-due who sends a check with deductions, you have something to fall back on. Some customers who are having financial problems will take deductions on old invoices as they pay them in order to appear less delinquent.

SENDING LETTERS TO PAST-DUE CUSTOMERS

Keep in mind that there may be state or federal requirements you must follow as you decide whether to buy or write your own collection letters. Here are some tips for writing letters that get you results.

- Speak or write in simple terms. Don't use big words or legal jargon if you can avoid it.
- Don't repeat yourself.
- Make sure that, after reading the letter, your customer knows everything you want them to know about your credit policy.
- Be sure your letter is compliant with any laws that might pertain to your business.
- Use clear language.
- Make sure the type or font is easy to read and not too small.
- Be organized with your thoughts as well as the call to action.

- Don't crowd or take up to much space; leave some white space.
- Be blunt and to the point while being professional.

If you have questions on any laws that might pertain to you and your collection efforts, you can show your letters to an attorney who is well versed on those laws. Be aware of the Uniform Consumer Credit Code (UCCC) as well as any changes to the Fair Debt Collection Practices Act and any laws of the state where you are and where your debtor is.

An important point to remember is that while collection letters—or dunning notices, as they are sometimes called—are effective and will help you collect more money, you need to use them in conjunction with your credit policy. Personal visits and/or phone calls should be an important part of your collection process in addition to dunning notices or collection letters.

Each letter must be written on your company letterhead and include your business's name, address, phone and fax numbers, Web address, e-mail, and any other contact information. The letters that get the best results are not form letters; documents like those lose some of their punch. Be sure to type your name and sign each letter, if possible, or use a signature stamp or cursive font in your word processing program.

Your letter should state in the first sentence your reason for sending it. Your second sentence should explain more about the first sentence, then suggest a solution and thank the recipient. The most effective letters are short, to the point, and easy to read; the more direct they are, the fewer misunderstandings you will have. Have other people read your letter and see if they totally understand it. If they do, then chances are your debtor will too.

Your letter is a reflection of your business, so keep it professional. Keep in mind that the goal of sending this document is to persuade someone to send you money. Your wording and tone are critical, especially if this is a customer with whom you want to continue to do business. Always assume the debtor will pay and enclose an envelope for payment, along with postage on the envelope if possible. The easier you make it for a debtor to make the payment, the better your chances are of receiving that payment.

Collection letters should do two things: retain customer good will and help you get paid. You know a letter works well when you send out mailings and your phone rings off the hook after everyone receives them. If, on the other hand, you send out a letter that gets no response, then you need to rework it.

SAMPLE COLLECTION LETTER

3-Letter Series

Letter #1—A Friendly Reminder Letter

Date

Dear _____,

Please be advised that your account has a past-due balance of $200 that was due on (date).

Please send your payment of $200 today in the enclosed payment envelope to bring your account current.

Please call this office at 000-000-0000 if there is a reason you have not paid this balance. Thank you for your prompt attention to this important matter.

Sincerely,

Letter #2—A Second Notice
Date

Dear _____,

We sent you a first notice on (date) requesting your payment of $200 to pay off your past-due balance on invoice #123. To date, we have not had a response or received your payment.

Your payment, or any questions you may have, should be directed to this office to ensure proper credit to your account. You may also pay online at www.MichelleDunn.com for your payment to be immediately credited to your account.

Sincerely,

Letter #3—A Final Notice
Date

Dear _____,

Because you have failed to respond to our previous letters, this is an attempt at an amicable resolution of your account.

Unless your payment reaches our office within the next seven (7) days, we will be forced to take further action. We urge you to send your payment today or call to pay by credit card. You can also pay online at www.MichelleDunn.com.

Toll free: 1-800-300-1234
[Your business mailing address]

We would like to resolve this matter and put it behind us as much as you would.

We are committed to taking whatever steps are necessary and proper to enforce payment of your obligation.

Sincerely,

Payment Plan Letter #1

Date

Dear _____,

This letter is to confirm the commitment you made during our telephone conversation. You stated that a check would be mailed on (date) in the amount of $200.00.

Thank you in advance for your payment.

Sincerely,

Payment Plan Letter #2

Date

Dear _____,

This letter is to confirm the commitment you made on the phone today. As agreed, you will send $25 a week starting Friday, November 4, 2011 by postal mail in the form of a check sent to (your business address). You will then send $25 every Friday until the balance is paid in full. Until this balance is paid, all new orders will be on a prepaid basis.

Enclosed please find a payment envelope for your first payment.

Sincerely,

5

DEBT COLLECTION CALLS

MAKING QUALITY COLLECTION CALLS

Making collection calls is a skill you develop from actually making the calls, reading all you can on how to do it, and listening to others who do it. You have to be able to anticipate what the customer is going to say and be ready for anything, and you must remain in control of the call. For your collection call to be a success it must always result in agreement as to what is to be done.

Use voice mail or answering machines if available. Leave detailed and complete messages, speak slowly, and always tell the customer what you want them to do. An example of a call to action could include returning your phone call by a certain time or date. Don't leave an open-ended message without any information or call to action.

From a business owner or employee standpoint, a collection call is "just one more damn thing" they have to do on a long list of things to do. Here are a few tips that will help you get your collection calls done quickly and efficiently.

- Schedule a regular time or day each week to make collection calls.
- Have all account information on hand.
- Leave messages, but do not reveal that the call is about an unpaid bill.
- Get the debtor to acknowledge the debt by asking if there was a question about the charge.
- Offer to take a credit card over the phone for payment.

- Ask when they will pay – and *wait for an answer*.
- Let them know you are documenting whatever commitment they make about a payment on their account.

You must ask questions that require specific answers when you are making collection calls. Speak with precision and make the transition from questions to a payment arrangement. Each question should be clear and to the point, with silence after each. An example:

Debtor: I can't pay; I don't have any money.

Collector: Are you working?

Debtor: Yes, but I just started a job and don't get paid for two weeks.

Collector: What day will you get paid?

Debtor: Friday.

Collector: On Saturday, you can mail me a money order for $25.

This scenario can go in a lot of different directions, depending on how the debtor responds. You have to be positive, confident, and compel them to agree to make a payment. Once you have come to an agreement, send them a confirmation letter with a payment envelope. Then call them on Friday to remind them to mail the payment the next day.

Keep in mind that the people from whom you are trying to get money will use a lot of excuses to avoid paying. I have had debtors tell me they did not receive the confirmation letter with the payment envelope and don't have any envelopes themselves, so they can't make the payment. You have to be ready for anything; you will never stop hearing new and different excuses. I told this particular customer that I could send her another payment envelope but I needed a new address so I could make sure she would receive it, and she could make two payments when she received it. The other option was taking a payment over the phone or Western Union that day.

There are several things you can do to make collection calls to past-due customers more effective. You want to get the most out of each call, because—let's face it—no one *likes* making collection calls. And customers certainly don't like receiving them.

Think about how you sound on the phone and work on developing your phone voice. You also want to refine your listening skills. It's always important to let the customer break the silence when you tell them you are calling about their past-due balance and that you want to be paid. This can be tough, but it gets easier and more effective the more you practice. I have done this for years, and believe me, the customer is more uncomfortable than you are with the silence, and will either respond or hang up quietly. Just give them a minute after you ask a question, and then wait.

You need to have some special skills that will help you be able to collect more money when making these kinds of calls. One of the most important traits is being a good communicator in person, on the phone, and in writing. The other most important trait is patience, in terms of your ability to ask questions, wait for an answer, and know when to be quiet and just listen. You will need to be persuasive and persistent, with the sensitivity to deal fairly with people in difficult situations. You must be able to stay calm under pressure, and be adaptable in delicate situations—for instance, when a debtor cries or swears at you. You must have strong negotiation skills and the ability to explain financial matters firmly and clearly. If you can do those things you should be able to collect more money than your average collector. Keep in mind that you need to have some type of office administrative skills so you can keep track of all the discussions you have with customers or debtors and any paperwork that might pertain to their past-due account. Computer skills are a must and can help streamline this process for you.

YOUR OPENING LINE

You will have already checked out the customer's account thoroughly when you pick up the phone to make a collection call. But do you have an opening line ready?

It is important that you never make a collection call without researching an account first. Check the information in your computer, make sure you know what the balance is for, when the last pay date was, which invoices make up the balance due, and if there were any disputes or problems with the order *before* you pick up the phone. Some things to look for before making a collection call are:

- The invoice number
- Date of the order, invoice, and shipment or service
- Total amount the customer owes and how much of that is past-due
- How many days past-due is the balance?
- The payment history
- Details of the order—purchase order number, shipping information, anything pertinent

- Have there been any disputes or comments added to this customer's account?
- Who placed the order?
- What did the customer tell you the last time you called asking them to pay?

When you make the call and a customer asks you anything about the account, you want to be prepared and have an answer. Being able to answer questions immediately increases your chances of being paid.

As I've previously emphasized, you have to be ready for some emotional reactions when you make calls to past-due customers. They might be angry, embarrassed, sad, or frustrated; they might cry, swear, and yell. Preparing yourself for these kinds of reactions is absolutely necessary. Making a debt collection call is hard enough without trying to convince a crying customer to send you money. It can seem strange that customers may get so upset about your call, especially considering that *they* owe *you* the money. However, debtors often feel as though companies can survive without getting paid and that they shouldn't have to pay if they are having hard times. When a debtor begins to tell you their life story and problems, you do need to display some empathy and compassion. But keep in mind that the purpose of your call is to get the bill paid. You can listen, let them know that you understand, and—based on their situation—offer a solution such as a payment plan or another option that will benefit both of you. This is not always easy or even possible to do, depending on the anger involved, but with some patience, it will work eventually.

FOUR TIPS TO IMPROVE YOUR PHONE DELIVERY

It is essential to convey confidence when speaking to customers about a past-due bill or discrepancy. You represent your company when you speak to a customer or anyone else with whom you do business; therefore, the way you talk, dress, and present yourself reflects upon your organization. What does your body or phone language say about you? Does it say you're trustworthy, confident, and competent—or just the opposite? Here are four simple tips for a confident phone voice that will help you to collect more money:

1. *Your Greeting*: Studies show that people make a judgment about you in the first two seconds of an interaction. It's not what you say in that short time that matters most, but often how you present yourself. A dull, monotone, "dead-fish" voice will leave your listener with little confidence in you or your message. Smile when you speak on the phone; it will be noticeable in your voice.

2. *Your Voice*: Sit up straight in your chair and picture the customer across the desk from you. When talking on the phone, imagine your audience sitting on the other side of your desk. Pay attention to how different your body language is. Do not slump in your chair, and notice how people react to you differently.

3. *Eye Contact*: Since there is no eye contact when you're on the phone, try to remain focused on the call and not on anything else going on around you. Think about how it feels when you are talking to someone who keeps looking around behind you to see what else is going on. Focus on your caller and be aware and alert.

4. *Confidence*: Think about former California Governor Arnold Schwarzenegger; he is a great example of someone who has an air of confidence about him. Regardless of the events surrounding him or the criticism he may encounter, he demonstrates poise. You won't see him wringing his hands, or rubbing them repeatedly through his hair, shuffling from foot to foot, jiggling the change in his pocket, or making nervous gestures. He comes across as someone who won't cower or retreat—just as a bill collector should act.

Pay attention to small, potentially distracting body movements, like tapping your toes, shaking your leg, fidgeting with your fingers, pens, or anything else. These are all signs of nervous energy. Look and sound more engaged and professional by channeling all that energy into your facial expression, voice, and posture.

6

USING E-MAIL IN COLLECTIONS

DIFFERENT TYPES OF E-MAIL

There are many different types of e-mail out there, the most common being Post Office Protocol or POP, Web-based e-mail, ISP mail services, Web site e-mail services, or mail forwarding services. No matter what type of e-mail service you or your customers use, they will be compatible. E-mail has become the "go to" form of communication in today's society.

PRIVATE E-MAIL

Your private e-mail account is the one you set up for personal correspondence with family or friends, which has nothing to do with your job or professional correspondence. E-mail may feel like a private one-on-one conversation, but in reality, it's only as confidential as talking out loud in a restaurant. E-mail messages can be intercepted and read anywhere in transit by anyone with the proper capabilities.

SOCIAL NETWORK E-MAIL

New statistics from Nielsen Online show that social networking had overtaken e-mail in terms of worldwide reach by the end of 2008. According to the study, 66.8 percent of Internet users across the globe accessed "member communities" last year, compared to 65.1 percent for e-mail. The most popular online activities remain search and Web portals (with around 85 percent each) and software manufacturers' websites.

The far-reaching study also explored a number of other trends within the social networking space. In 2008, users spent 63 percent more time on member communities than they did in the previous year. However, within member communities, Facebook saw growth of 566 percent in time spent on it by users worldwide. As has been reported elsewhere, Facebook's fastest growth demographic is older users—the social network acquired 12.4 million people between ages 35 to 49 in 2008, according to Nielsen.

USING E-MAIL TO COMMUNICATE WITH YOUR CUSTOMERS

Collectors are eager to use new technologies—such as e-mail, instant messages, and texting—as tools to provide collection notices, verification, and messages to debtors. The Federal Trade Commission (FTC) states that it is not aware of any information demonstrating that third parties have greater access to debt collection messages conveyed through online methods rather than traditional means (phone calls and letters). Additionally, the FTC does not believe that the imposition of any special limitations on debt collectors' use of e-mail and instant messages is justified. However, they do feel that if a third party becomes aware of a debt through any method—such as e-mail or instant messaging—the collector is and will be held liable for violating Section 805(b) of the FDCPA.

Some debtors are more receptive to e-mails as a form of communication and will make that known to you as the collector. More and more people spend time on their computers and have e-mails going directly to their cell phones, so they may ask you to communicate this way with them. If a debtor states that this is the preferred way of communication and provides you with an e-mail address, just be sure to keep that information in writing in their file. Also, include the Mini Miranda if you are a third party collector at the end of each e-mail message.

The Mini Miranda informs the consumer that the letter or call is from a debt collector, that they are contacting the consumer in order to collect a debt, and that any information revealed or obtained during the call will be used for that purpose. The Mini Miranda is a provision of the Fair Debt Collection Practices Act to prevent debt collectors from calling under false pretenses in order to gain information from a consumer to be used against them.

The use of e-mail risks third party disclosure under the Fair Debt Collection Practices Act. Since e-mail can be electronically stored at several locations—such as where it originates and where it is sent—it's not considered a secure form of communication. Something to keep in mind when considering using e-mail to communicate about debt collection is that many employers monitor employee e-mail accounts and usage; some consumers and businesses even have employees that check their e-mails for them. Most medium-sized or large organizations generally have their own e-mail servers. It's usually best to keep personal correspondence away from this business e-mail ID. Company e-mail addresses have many strings attached, so employees have to be wary of how and what they use them for. If an organization uses an electronic mail system, the employer owns it and is allowed to review its contents. New technologies make it possible for employers to monitor many aspects of their employees' jobs, especially on telephones, computer terminals, through electronic and voice mail, and via Internet use, and this kind of monitoring is virtually unregulated. Therefore, unless company policy specifically states otherwise (and even this is not assured), employers may listen, watch, and read most of staff members' workplace communications.

Messages sent within the company as well as those that are sent from your terminal to another company—or from another company to you—are subject to monitoring by your employer. This includes Web-based e-mail accounts such as Yahoo! and Hotmail, as well as instant messages and voice mail systems. Employees should *not* assume that these activities are private and unsupervised. There have actually been several workplace privacy court cases that were decided in the employer's favor.

There are two states—Connecticut and Delaware—that require employers to give notice to an employee prior to monitoring their e-mail communications. Colorado and Tennessee require states to adopt a policy regarding monitoring public employees' e-mail accounts. Your boss—or you, if you're the boss—has the legal right to check any e-mail that is sent via your work address. For these reasons, you must make sure you have covered all aspects of disclosure requirements imposed by the FDCPA and/or your state's laws when using e-mail as a form of debt collection communication. I suggest that you create policies and procedures specifically focused on e-mail and how it can or will be used in your organization. Some things to consider including in these guidelines are:

- Customer authorization in writing to communicate via e-mail.
- Utilizing e-mail only when it is initiated by the debtor or customer.

Consider the age bracket of the people who owe you money when deciding upon methods of communication for bill collection. If you have a younger customer base, they are likely to respond better to e-mail since it is more convenient and less confrontational. Younger generations also tend to be more invested in technology than older customers who may not even use computers. However, don't make this assumption; some older generations might prefer receiving e-mail or text. The best idea is to check with individual customers and see what works best for them. Remember: You always want to use the method that will help you get paid the fastest!

WHAT YOU CAN DO

If you decide to use e-mail as a means of corresponding with your past-due customers, make sure the e-mail address you are using belongs to that person *exclusively*. And keep in mind that even if this is the case, you have no control over when or where the e-mail will be read, which can bring up a privacy concern. Be sure to have permission (written is best) with your customers to correspond regarding past-due balances through e-mail.

WHAT YOU *CAN'T* DO

There aren't currently any laws that forbid companies to utilize e-mail—either private or at work—as a communication tool with customers. But you must use common sense when you decide whether you want to take this route. Some questions to ask yourself when you consider using e-mail for collections:

- How will you verify that this e-mail address belongs exclusively to that customer or debtor?
- Will a third party ever see the e-mail?
- Are you sure the debtor receives the e-mails in a timely manner? How often do they check their e-mail, and is there any way to determine this?

Using e-mail as a collection tool is really based on personal preference; if you feel it will be effective for your billing department, you might want to set up a few rules and do a trial run. This will help you gauge whether it will work for your business, by seeing whether it increases your bottom line or by whether you receive more responses when you send out a past-due bill by e-mail.

Because contacting debtors via e-mail allows the recipient to avoid confrontation, many customers will be receptive to receiving past-due notices, statements, or invoices by e-mail. Many like this method because they don't have to explain why they are past-due if you e-mail them, whereas if you call them, they are put on the spot and need to provide an answer right then.

OBTAINING CONSENT TO USE E-MAIL

Two states, Nevada and Minnesota, require that Internet service providers keep certain information private unless the customer gives disclosure permission. Both of these states prohibit disclosure of any personally identifying information, but Minnesota also requires ISPs to get permission from customers before disclosing information about their online habits. (Minnesota statute 325M.01 to .09 & Nevada revised statute 205.498)

LAWS PERTAINING TO E-MAIL

Americans have always expressed great concerns about privacy on the Internet, concerns to which state legislatures have responded in several ways. Some state-level actions that are directly related to Internet privacy include laws that cover:

- Privacy of personal information
- Employee e-mail communications
- Privacy policies

The FDCPA does not cover online technology in reference to debt collection. We are hopeful that, as the FDCPA is updated and changes are made, online collection techniques and technology will be specifically addressed.

I would like to bring to your attention a portion of the February 2009 Federal Trade Commission workshop report:

> Consumer advocates expressed serious misgivings about the possible consumer harm that might arise if debt collectors were free to contact consumers via mobile phones and other newer technology methods.

These commentators noted three primary concerns:
1. That some of these methods, such as mobile telephones, e-mail, text messages, and instant messaging, may lack

the requisite level of data security or confidentiality to be used for sensitive debt collection matters.

2. That consumers may incur costs for some contacts using new technologies if, for example, the mobile calling plan of a consumer who receives a debt collection call does not permit unlimited minutes, or imposes charges for text messages.

3. That debt collectors using newer technologies may inconvenience or embarrass consumers by contacting them when they are driving, in appointments, or at work.

It is my understanding that FTC roundtables currently taking place will provide a stepping-stone to FDCPA reform. The FTC has concluded that major problems exist in the flow of information within the debt collection system, and that they need to modernize debt collection laws to take into account the changes in technology that have occurred since the laws were put in place.

The FDCPA does not apply to creditors or businesses that are collecting their own debts in their own name. If you, as a business, extend credit, you are authorized to pursue its collection. This, of course, does not mean creditors can do anything they want in order to collect; they must be aware of privacy laws, harassment, or defamation when collecting on any debt that is owed to them. As an example, if you as a creditor call late at night to a customer who owes you money, or call repeatedly at work or home and make threats, you'll find yourself in legal hot water. You have to temper any aggressive language or behavior in order to avoid a lawsuit. As long as you stay within the boundaries and use common sense, you shouldn't have a problem.

CAN-SPAM RULES

The Federal Trade commission enforces a law that sets rules for commercial e-mail, establishes requirements for commercial messages, gives recipients the right to have you stop e-mailing them, and spells out tough penalties for violations. Despite its name, the CAN-SPAM Act doesn't apply just to bulk e-mail. It covers all commercial messages, which the law defines as "any electronic mail message the primary purpose of which is the commercial advertisement or promotion of a commercial product or service," including e-mail that promotes content on commercial websites. The law makes no exception for business-to-business e-mail. That means all e-mail—for example, a message to former customers announcing a new product line—must comply with the law.

If you use e-mail in your business, you need to be familiar with this law, since it sets the rules for commercial e-mail; establishes requirements for these kinds of messages; gives recipients the right to have you stop e-mailing them (even if they owe you money); and spells out tough penalties for any violations.

Each separate e-mail in violation of the CAN-SPAM Act is subject to penalties of up to $16,000, making non-compliance very costly. However, following the law isn't complicated; here's a rundown of CAN-SPAM's main requirements.

1. *Don't use false or misleading header information.* Your "From," "To," "Reply To," and routing information— including the originating domain name and e-mail

address—must be accurate and identify the person or business who initiated the message.

2. *Don't use deceptive subject lines.* The subject line must accurately reflect the message's content.

3. *You must identify the message as an advertisement.* The law gives you a lot of leeway in how to do this, but you must disclose clearly and conspicuously that your message is indeed an advertisement.

4. *Tell recipients where you are located.* Your message must include your valid, physical postal address. This can be your current street address, a post office box you've registered with the U.S. Postal Service, or a private mailbox you've registered with a commercial mail-receiving agency established under Postal Service regulations.

5. *Tell recipients how to opt-out of receiving future e-mail from you.* Your message must include a clear and conspicuous explanation of how the recipient can opt-out of getting e-mail from you in the future. Craft the notice in a way that's easy for an ordinary person to recognize, read, and understand; you can improve clarity by creatively using type size, color, and location. Give a return e-mail address or another easy, Internet-based way to allow people to communicate their choice to you. You may want to create a menu to allow recipients to opt-out of certain types of messages while still receiving others; however, you must include the option to stop all commercial messages from you. And make sure your spam filter doesn't block these opt-out requests.

6. *Honor opt-out requests promptly.* Any opt-out mechanism you offer must be able to process the opt-out requests for at least 30 days after you send your

message, and you must honor the request within 10 business days. You can't charge a fee, require the recipient to give you any personally identifying information beyond an e-mail address, or make the recipient take any step other than sending a reply e-mail or visiting a single page on an Internet website as a condition for honoring their request. Once people have told you they don't want to receive more messages from you, you can't sell or transfer their e-mail addresses, even in the form of a mailing list. The only exception is that you may transfer the addresses to a company you've hired to help you comply with the CAN-SPAM Act.

7. *Monitor what others are doing on your behalf.* The law makes clear that even if you hire another company to handle your e-mail marketing, you can't contract away your legal responsibility to comply with the law. Both the company whose product is promoted in the message and the one that actually sends the message may be held legally responsible.

This information is taken from the Federal Trade Commission's Compliance Guide for Businesses. More information can be found on their website at http://business. ftc.gov/documents/bus61-can-spam-act-Compliance-Guide-for-Business.

THE FEDERAL TRADE COMMISSION

The FTC realizes that the debt collection laws that are in place now are old and outdated and don't reflect today's technology, such as the Internet, cell phones, caller ID, or text messages.

For that reason, you need to pay attention to the CAN-SPAM Act until other laws are updated.

The Fair Debt Collection Practices Act

The FTC enforces the FDCPA, or Fair Debt Collection Practices Act, and the FCRA as well as other federal laws that collectors must follow. The FDCPA—which is the law that regulates the debt collection industry—does not prohibit the use of e-mail in collecting debts. However, this is only because the law is outdated and does not specify the form of communication that can be used. This law was written based on the forms of communication that were available at that time, and although times have changed, many laws haven't changed with them. You can certainly use common sense, though, and assume that any FDCPA mention of communication also includes any new type of communication that is not yet covered, since it will be when the law is changed. Since e-mail is similar to postal mail, apply any postal mail laws to any e-mails you send out. Also, remember that the FDCPA only applies to third party collectors, so if you are a business owner or a credit manager working for a company collecting debts, this law does not pertain to you. The FDCPA also only applies to consumer debts, not business-to business-debts.

One credit and collections professional with whom I spoke, who has more than 25 years experience in this industry, thinks e-mailing invoices is effective; however, she isn't so sure about e-mailing overdue notices.

Some credit managers have indicated that their staff has been cut due to the implementation of e-mailing customers with an overdue letter or notice. They don't see an increase in response or payments, and they feel that phone calls are still the most effective way to get paid on a past-due bill.

An interesting case study might be to look at Australia, where using an e-mail address is allowed as long as you have verified that it is the correct debtor's e-mail address. Additionally, senders must be very careful when using employer or work e-mails due to the aforementioned possibility of third party access. One Australian credit manager with whom I spoke will only e-mail a customer or debtor if they e-mail her first. If that is the case, they use that e-mail address to send payment reminders by e-mail. By doing this, they've increased their payment arrangements with past-due customers by more than 15 percent.

One of the most common ways that larger companies protect their e-mails is by encrypting e-mail messages. To do this, they use software to scramble the messages, which the recipient then unscrambles to read.

I recently had a collector e-mail me to ask me what the law is on e-mailing debtors regarding overdue accounts. She told me that although many of her company's clients have given them e-mail addresses, they aren't sure if they can legally communicate this way. Another collector told me that they receive e-mail addresses from consumers as well, and she strongly advised against communicating via e-mails, especially unsolicited communications. Some collectors inform consumers who ask to be contacted by e-mail that they are legally unable to accommodate their request. If the collection issue is a commercial collection, many collectors will communicate via e-mail since the Fair Debt Collection Practices Act does not apply. Unless you take steps to encrypt your e-mail, don't count on e-mail as a confidential way of corresponding with anyone.

HACKING AND IDENTITY THEFT

If you send e-mails from a home-based business, or for your company while you're at home, you run the risk that anonymous hackers will intercept them. If you are suspected of any crime, law enforcement can seize your e-mails with a warrant. An e-mail thief can convince others that any communication is from a legitimate business. Therefore, business e-mail addresses are often stolen. If you think a communication is from a legitimate company, then you are more likely to share personal details with them. This is known as phishing.

Another reason to steal identity is in order to send spam, most of which will be blocked by the Internet Service Provider (ISP). Someone perpetrating e-mail identity theft can send an e-mail to an individual or firm under the guise of someone legitimate, therefore making it less likely to be blocked. If you have an irate customer who may be unhappy about being contacted by e-mail about a past-due debt, they may report your e-mail as spam.

As a business owner, you primarily use e-mail addresses to contact and communicate with your customers, past-due or not. So how can you protect your company e-mail from identity theft or from being marked as spam by your past-due customers that don't want to hear from you by e-mail? Try adopting some of the following tactics to stop your business from being accused of spamming.

- Avoid being blocked yourself by using a different domain registrar from that of the Web hosting company.

- Think about using a second hosting company just in case anything goes wrong and you are blocked. This second account can be your backup service.
- Don't share an IP address (shared hosting), because your e-mail will also be blocked if someone you are sharing with gets blocked for spamming.

SENDING INVOICES VIA E-MAIL

A Romanian member of my American Credit & Collections Association sends unpaid invoices through e-mail. Some businesses offer customers the ability to view and find unpaid invoices on the Web. Other agencies based in the United States are using online websites for skiptracing, and some agencies I have talked to have improved their results 25 to 30 percent once they started doing this. Clearly, many companies are becoming more comfortable and adept at using these electronic communication methods to get the money owed to them. You just want to make sure that you're doing it as efficiently as possible, and following the rules every step of the way.

DO I NEED PERMISSION?

I've found as a creditor that many debtors prefer to receive text messages and e-mails, and that they are also the most effective way to increase collections. In fact, one company I know has experienced a 12 percent lift in communication by using these methods. It seems that debtors perceive these avenues of communication to be less invasive than a phone call. They also give your customers the sense that they have control over when and if they respond (which can be both a positive and negative thing).

Some collectors with whom I have spoken obtain consent from their customers to use text messages for future correspondence even before the sale takes place. They include wording such as the following on the paperwork the customer signs when opening an account, such as the credit application, agreement, or contract: *"By signing this document, customer agrees to accept and understands that text messages may be used when servicing their account, including the collecting of debts."*

Others have taken it a step further by providing a more detailed outline of how text messages will be used. They always get the customer to sign and acknowledge this provision: *"You authorize us (your company name) to send you (customer name) a text message at any mobile number at which we reasonably believe we can contact you, for any lawful purpose, including but not limited to:*

1. *Suspected fraud or identity theft*
2. *Obtaining information necessary to service your account*
3. *Collecting on your account*
4. *Notifying you about important issues regarding your account"*

It's vital to remember, if you are thinking of doing this, that—once again—all messages must include a mechanism for the consumer to opt-out of receiving further text messages at any time. This is to protect the consumer and the collector, especially since the law does not specifically address text messages being sent as a form of dunning. If you decide to send text messages about bills to your customers, make sure the customer is not charged for the text and that you as the company incur that charge. Also consider the fact that some cell phones that accept text messages may be business phones provided by a consumer's employer. In these cases, that employer may have the right to view any text messages sent to or received by that company phone. This would violate third party disclosure through the FDCPA. Also, many consumers have phones that multiple family members may use, and anyone might see a message from you meant for a sibling or parent.

Another item to think about when using text messages is: How much space are you going to use to include the Mini Miranda (if you are a third party collector) or your collection information? It may be difficult to include any legal information along with a debt collection notice on the limited character count that a text message gives you.

You might want to take a look at the Telephone Consumer Protection Act (TCPA) since their requirements may also apply to text messages. The TCPA prohibits any call using any type of automated dialing telephone system to any number assigned through a cellular telephone service. If you are using an automatic dialer, be sure to verify you aren't breaking any laws.

The following are some steps you can take to protect yourself and avoid getting into trouble. Keep in mind, however, that these are not complete, since the law is not entirely clear on this issue.

- Obtain consent from the consumer in writing to communicate via e-mail or text.
- Clearly state in your e-mails or text messages that you are a bill collector.
- Include your phone number.

- Provide opt-out information so a consumer can stop any e-mails or text messages.
- Use "Free to end user" services so debtors or consumers never incur a charge for your messages.

SENDING ATTACHMENTS

Most folks who receive an attachment on an e-mail from someone they don't know will not open that attachment. I know that *I* don't do so unless I know it's coming and I'm sure of who is sending it. Many e-mail attachments are viruses or worms that can immediately infect a computer once opened. Some folks have their e-mail program set up not to accept an e-mail with an attachment, or to receive the e-mail without the attachment. In light of this information, you might want to imbed your invoice or notice into the body of the e-mail in order for the recipient to be able to receive and view it.

Some companies simply send an e-mail alert to their customers when they have an invoice or statement ready to be viewed and paid. This may be a better alternative for you if you are worried about security or sending attachments. You can send a link to the customers' invoices and statements, so that they just get an e-mail with a link to click that takes them to a secure page. This page can then show their payment and order history, a specific invoice, or their monthly statement.

Accounting software such as QuickBooks, Peachtree, or Quicken also gives you the option to send statements through that program. This might be a better option for you and your customers. Check with your software to see what your options are in regards to sending statements directly from QuickBooks.

DO I NEED PERMISSION?

While you don't legally need permission to send invoices this way, realistically, you should ask for it. Not only does it protect your business, it also keeps a good line of communication open with your customers. Just because a certain individual is currently past-due doesn't mean they will continue to be so, or fail to be a loyal and reliable customer in the future. To maintain first-rate customer relations, ask for permission to use e-mail as a form of communication before you just launch into e-mailing invoices, statements, or past-due notices.

VERIFYING DELIVERY

Some e-mail programs offer the option of a return receipt. This is extremely helpful if you are looking for a way to be sure the e-mail was sent and delivered—and maybe even opened and read. There are different software packages available for a fee that will do this for you. Since I have not used any of them myself, I cannot give you a recommendation; however, I can provide some information on the few of which I'm aware.

eTracker is a service that confirms your e-mail delivery status. The eTracker Agent program allows you to access the eTracker service, which includes the ability to create a list of contacts, monitor delivery status, and receive readers' information. eTracker Agent can answer the following questions:

- Does your recipient read your e-mail?
- When/how many times does he/she read?
- What is the recipient's IP address and OS information?

There is also a program called ReadNotify that lets you know when an e-mail you've sent gets read. Their website is: http://www.readnotify.com.

As with anything else, you should research any of these companies before you pay for software. Get recommendations and references, and talk to people who use the service.

CORRESPONDING THROUGH E-MAIL ABOUT PAST-DUE ACCOUNTS

You might want to design a form e-mail with options to be used when you e-mail past-due or dunning notices to delinquent customers. You may also want to have permission to contact your customer through e-mail in these instances. If, for example, you make collection calls and get a "voice mailbox full" message, you may want to try e-mailing. Begin your e-mail by letting the customer know that you tried to call but the message box was full. You can just have a standard e-mail letter and cut and paste it into the body of an e-mail; for example, if someone gave you a credit card payment that's being denied, you could send something as simple as, "Your credit card payment has been denied. To avoid any interruption in service, please update your billing information right away." You could then go on to offer them options on updating their billing information and/or making a payment directly by calling you, by mail, or online. Here is an example of these step-by-step instructions.

1. Your Payment Schedule shows a list of your active services. Those with past-due payments are marked with a past-due alert.

2. Click the "Update your payment method" link in the past-due alert.

3. To edit the credit card you are currently using to pay for your service, click "Edit." To switch to a new payment method, click the "Add a new payment method" link in the upper-right corner of the page. Be sure to click "Continue" to save your changes.

SENDING BACKUP DOCUMENTATION THROUGH E-MAIL

This brings us back to the attachment problem. Since many people won't open an attachment about which they haven't been warned, it's best to let your recipients know that you're sending the backup documentation they requested as an e-mail attachment. You can then send the e-mail and follow up with a phone call right away to tell them you sent it—and then hold while they open it.

Another option is faxing the documents. Many folks receive faxes right on their computer, so when you fax something they can open it and look at it without printing it if they don't need to.

PROOF OF DELIVERY

Proof of delivery (POD) is most often requested by the customer. If they claim to have never received the item, you have to get evidence that it was delivered from the shipper. You can frequently have the shipper send the proof of delivery by e-mail, fax, or mail directly to your customer. The most important part about doing this is following up, making a call as soon as you know the proof of delivery has been sent.

It is sometimes harder for a debtor to claim they didn't get something from you and also didn't get the POD from the shipper. In these instances, they know they are really stretching it and may end up just trying to avoid you. This is usually a confirmation of guilt; you know they received the product, the POD, and the notices. In my experience, they will avoid you because they know they are caught in a lie, but they will mail the check without speaking to anyone in order to avoid a confrontation. Many times they just avoid you completely and never pay.

PROOF OF SALE OR ORDER

Some collectors send e-mails to debtors only in reply to an e-mail received by a debtor—and only if the debtor is asking for a copy of an invoice, a release or paid in full letter, or some other document. When they do this, they follow up with the debtor within 30 minutes of sending the e-mail with the attachment containing the requested information. Remember that collectors have a legal obligation to provide information to support a debt or claim of a debt they make to a consumer.

DUNNING NOTICES

Imagine the benefits of saving time and money that we would reap if we could communicate securely and effectively with debtors via e-mail. Postage stamps are up to 44 cents, and the notion of becoming greener and saving paper by not using "snail mail" sounds great. There seem to be many advantages. However, with the amount of sue-happy consumers and attorneys out there, I would be leery of completely embracing the e-mail approach until laws are changed and specific regulations are in place regarding online communications with debtors in any form.

Debt collectors do, however, need to utilize new communication technologies to contact consumers, since doing so makes their collection efforts easier and more efficient. These new means of exchange offer contact methods that will increasingly become the norm. Any restrictions on the ability of collectors to contact consumers using new technologies will increase the amount of debt that goes uncollected—a topic to be addressed in the next roundtable discussion by the FTC.

When Congress enacted the FDCPA, it did not limit the methods a debt collector could use to contact a consumer except for prohibiting the use of postcards, but this was before any new technology. However, it is important to remember that the FDCPA was enacted to prevent debt collectors from engaging in unfair, deceptive, or abusive conduct while using any method to collect a debt. New technology raises questions and issues not considered when the FDCPA was enacted.

FINAL NOTICE BEFORE FURTHER ACTION

While you can certainly send a final notice letter through e-mail, I wouldn't recommend taking this approach. This is because it is much too easy for the debtor to claim they never saw it. Unless you use a company that offers a receipt or proof of delivery on that e-mail, I would send the final notice by priority mail or certified mail and also send a copy through the regular postal mail to ensure delivery. Include this wording on the bottom of your final notice: "A copy of this notice has also been sent by regular postal mail to ensure delivery." I used priority mail with delivery confirmation in the past. There have also been some occasions when I have used certified mail and had to take debtors to court. They claimed they did not receive the notice, and the judges have always ruled in my favor because of this clause. A judge told me to add this to the correspondence in order to win my cases in court. It has always worked for me and can't hurt for you to try.

7

USING SOCIAL MEDIA IN COLLECTIONS

WHAT ARE ONLINE COLLECTION TECHNIQUES?

Online collection techniques are skills that collectors use to locate debtors on the Internet to try to collect on a debt.

In late 2007, the Federal Trade Commission held a public workshop to evaluate the need for changes in the debt collection system, including the FDCPA, in order to protect consumers better. The goal of this two-day workshop was to explore changes in the collection industry and examine their impact on consumers and businesses. Based on the results they found during those 48 hours, the FTC concluded that the debt collection legal system needs to be reformed and modernized to reflect changes in consumer debt, the debt collection industry, and technology, while protecting consumers and without unduly burdening the debt collection industry.

In my experience, technology continues to change the debt collection environment by solving problems, enhancing debt collection processes, and automating functions. Most new tools make processes more cost effective and efficient, since, the Internet has forced collectors to be educated and actively involved online. Some examples of types of online collection websites are skiptracing websites, such as searchamerica.com, Merlin data, court records, or anything online that can help a collector locate a debtor.

Consumer credit is a critical part of today's economy, whether it is good or bad. Credit allows consumers to purchase goods and services for which they are unable or unwilling to pay the entire cost at the time of their purchase. Extending credit requires creditors to take the risk that the consumer will not be able to repay all or part of the money they owe. If consumers do not pay their bills, creditors will become less willing to take on that risk, and may be more likely to increase the cost of extending credit.

Technological innovations have given debt collectors more efficient and effective methods for tracking and contacting consumers. The FTC believes that there are two major problems with the flow of information from creditors to debt collectors and from debt collectors to the consumer. The first is that debt collectors often have inadequate information when they contact consumers, which increases the likelihood that they will reach the wrong consumer and try to collect the wrong amount. The second is that the debt collectors do not provide adequate information to the consumer. This makes it more difficult for consumers to assess whether they actually owe the debt in question and should exercise their rights under the FDCPA.

There are many databases that allow people to register, join, and use their services to locate debtors. There are others that provide information on bankruptcy filings or whether a debtor is deceased.

Some collectors have reported finding a debtor's location information in a news story or by Googling a name and checking out social networking pages. You could also set up Google Alerts for a specific name if you are having trouble finding that person; Google will then e-mail you each time that name is mentioned somewhere on the Web. Additionally, many local and national newspapers have their publications available online, so you can receive an alert if the person you're seeking is mentioned in any story.

According to the February 2009 workshop report by the Federal Trade Commission, database technology has changed the techniques that creditors and debt collectors use to find consumers. As recently as 20 years ago, collectors' attempts to locate a consumer were limited to calling references, trying to find neighbors through reverse-look-up directories, or visiting consumers in person. Nowadays, you can obtain location information by accessing huge electronic databases that collect consumer information such as telephone numbers, social security numbers, real estate records, court records, marriage records, addresses, names of relatives, and others living at the same address. Free telephone directories are also available on the Internet, providing information nationwide. Some databases also provide information on whether a debtor has filed or been discharged from bankruptcy proceedings or is deceased.

FINDING DEBTORS USING SOCIAL NETWORKING WEBSITES

Social networking sites are venues where people can exchange personal or business information with others through a forum specifically designed to make it easy to share text, pictures, documents, music, videos, and other data and comments. There are thousands of social networking sites out there today; some focus on particular industries, interests, subjects, or topics. Members can join most of them for free, create a profile, and add anything they would like. They also use them to connect with other like-minded people who are also members.

Many collectors nowadays use social networks to find debtors, since many debtors have public profile pages on social sites. Collectors can use these to find e-mail and mailing addresses, as well as home and cell phone numbers, places of employment, and other contact information. Collectors also utilize other online tools to locate debtors and verify information—tools such as search engines, blogs, message boards, posted videos, newsgroups, and photos.

Social media tools are used every day by collectors, more frequently as skiptracing tools than as a way to actually collect a debt. While sites such as Twitter, Facebook, or LinkedIn can help to locate a debtor, using any one of those websites to announce any type of pending or ongoing collection activity would violate the FDCPA in a multitude of ways. Utilizing social networking sites to gather information and investigate a person's history requires a lot of work; even when it is successful, it often will give you only a single chance at getting a payment.

Many social media sites are geared towards certain audiences. LinkedIn is designed for business people wanting to network, while MySpace is focused on a younger crowd. One collector I know joined MySpace to search for her past-due customers that were under 30 years old. It's important to know what demographics are using what sites. If you are looking for a target group of debtors within the same age group, you can look at the many social networking sites to see where your specific customers or debtors hang out. Remember when you're checking out the profiles that these individuals may have links on their social networking page to other websites or blogs in which they participate, and you may be able to use them to gather more information.

THINGS YOU CAN FIND ON SOCIAL NETWORKS THAT CAN HELP YOU AS A COLLECTOR

The first thing many collectors do in order to locate a debtor or get information is visit social networks. People make themselves very easy to find these days, and they post all kinds of personal information that is helpful in tracking them down. Some pieces of valuable information you can find posted on social networks are:

- Birth date
- Address
- Employment information
- Asset information

Just a name and a birth date allow a collector to search public records on any individual. Each social networking site differs in terms of the specific information they offer and processes by which you can search. I discuss a few in details in the next sections.

FACEBOOK

Many people have asked me what you can find on each specific social site. Since I am not familiar with all of them in detail—and don't know what the inquiring individuals are looking for—I recommend that you simply begin with the basics. A Facebook profile can include some of the following information, depending on whether the person is a "friend" and what level of privacy settings they have established.

- What someone looks like (depending on what they've chosen for a profile photo).
- Their current city and state.
- Their friends—you can see if there are any "mutual" acquaintances to connect you.
- Their "likes" and other pages to which they've linked.
- Links to other social networks in which they participate.
- Their status or updates, which might include information about when and where they spend money, get a new job, buy a house, or get a raise or bonus.

You can then click on the tabs at the top of the profile for more information. For example, if you click on *Info,* you can possibly discover a hometown city and state; information about or links to siblings, relatives, or significant others; an e-mail address, IM name, or physical or mailing address; and an employer and where it is located. Some people have all kinds of photos available as well, so if you are trying to serve them any legal papers, you now know what they look like. While not everyone provides all of this information, you will be surprised at how many do so in great detail.

It is worth mentioning that in December 2008, the Supreme Court of the Australian Capital Territory ruled that Facebook is a valid protocol for serving court notices to defendants. It is believed to be the world's first legal judgment that defines a summons posted on Facebook as legally binding. And in March 2009, New Zealand High Court associate justice David Glendall allowed for the serving of legal papers on Craig Axe by the company Axe Market Garden via Facebook.

Never forget that your customers, colleagues, clients, managers, and investors are on Facebook, Twitter, LinkedIn, or other social networking websites too. In fact, 78 percent of retailers surveyed by the e-tailing group, inc. have a Facebook page, and 64 percent have a Twitter account.

MYSPACE

When you look on MySpace for a debtor's name, make sure to try to narrow your search by using the form on the right hand side. Here, you can input the city and state if you know them, zip code, gender, age, and more. Since there are so many people with the same name, you want to make sure you always have the right person. When you visit someone's MySpace profile, you will immediately see a picture (usually of the person). They often list their age, gender, city, state, and country next to that picture, as well as whatever they have written about themselves and their lives. This can include information about their jobs, can tell you if they own anything, or are moving, buying a car, or making any other substantial purchases or decisions in their lives. This can help when you are making collection calls, because they are probably telling you the truth if what they offer matches what you've seen on MySpace. If you keep looking down the left hand side of the profile you can also find their occupation, which can help you as you search for places of employment. You can also discover a user's education and employment history as long as they filled that portion out.

TWITTER

Twitter is a social networking website that allows its users to share and discover what is happening right this moment, anywhere in the world. More and more companies and brands are joining the Twitter network. The site gives anyone who signs up the ability to send and read messages known as *tweets*, which are text posts of up to 140 characters displayed on that user's profile page and on the pages of their followers. Most people use Twitter to communicate or keep in touch with friends and family by telling them what they are doing or asking questions. Many also use the site to follow brands in which they have an interest, and to find out about special events, deals, sales, or new products.

Using Twitter to locate a debtor can result in a photo, name of city and state, possibly a website if they have one, or perhaps an employer's website. You can read their tweets to see what they have been up to and where they have been. Are they looking for a job, buying a car, or going through bankruptcy? Are they currently out of the state or country? Are they dealing with other difficult personal, professional, or financial issues?

While the Twitter search tool actually isn't the best way to find people on Twitter, it is a good start. Just click on "Find People" at the top of the page and insert the name of the person you are looking for. Although you can search for people's names through Twitter, there are also other ways to search.

You can also use a website like Tweepz, which lets you limit searches to specific parts of Twitter's user information (like name, bio, and location). Additionally, you can filter results by follower/following numbers, location, and other terms to greatly improve on your results. Another Twitter search tool is called TweepSearch, which lets you search by Twitter name, location, or a specific username.

SOCIAL MEDIA SUCCESS TIPS

The following are my top four tips on how to most effectively use social networks to locate debtors and improve your business.

- Don't worry or analyze too much about taking the social media plunge. This is one time when you should follow the pack and participate in what everyone else is doing.
- As with any networking event—listen before you "talk."
- Track conversations with keywords as well as personal, company, and executives' names. Use Google Reader and Google Blog Search (both free tools) to track them.
- Practice participating in various social media sites so that you understand how they work. Many potential debtors spend hours on these websites and know them inside out.

The following are a few oft-repeated myths about social media.

- *It's a passing fad.* Social media is here to stay and growing every day.
- *It is something you can control.* Users control social media, not the viewers. You can only control your reaction.
- *It only requires a one-time set up.* You cannot just set up a profile or join a social media site and leave it, and then expect to reap the benefits. You must be active and log into your account. Social media is something you have to work at and keep learning about for it to be effective.

- *There are no rules.* Some people believe they can do and say whatever they want without consequences. This certainly isn't the case on social media sites or anywhere else (although it may help you locate debtors or businesses that owe money).

8

THIRD PARTY
COLLECTION
SERVICES

Many people think collection agencies are out there just trying to make a buck at a consumer's expense. However, a collection agency is a service business, just like a dry cleaner. Companies hire collection agencies when they don't get paid, and expect them to collect from the debtor and send the money, less their charges, back to the company.

When I started my collection agency, I wasn't thinking about how I could squeeze money out of people with no cash so that I could have more cash. I did it because I had worked as an accounts receivable clerk and as a credit manager for many years and I had experience in this field. Starting my agency allowed me to have flexibility with my work schedule so that I could be available for my children. I, of course, hoped to make money doing this, but I didn't want it to happen by harassing people, yelling at them, or breaking laws. I hadn't done that as a credit manager and didn't plan to do that as an agency owner.

The feelings many consumers have about debt makes it easier for them to blame or be angry at whoever is asking them to pay their bills. But how does it make you feel when you have to repeatedly call or visit someone who owes you money in order to get paid? Is it fair for the person who owes you money to be angry at you and yell and swear at you in addition to not paying you? You did them a favor by offering them credit and now you are the bad guy—simply because you want to be paid. When you look at it this way, you see that collection agencies and agents aren't the evil forces they're often made out to be.

HOW TO CHOOSE A COLLECTION AGENCY

Choosing a professional collection service to manage delinquent accounts and other related tasks is a significant decision. The agency should represent your organization in a responsible and professional manner and provide a satisfactory rate of recovery while maintaining your public image. This decision involves more than just giving your business to the lowest bidder; it requires careful consideration.

To that end, you'll want to ask yourself the following questions when choosing an outside or third-party collection agency.

- Is the agency a member of a national trade association? Such membership is an indication of professional integrity and you can contact the trade association for a reference.
- Does the agency belong to a local Chamber of Commerce, Better Business Bureau, Rotary Club, or any other networking group that you can contact for a reference?
- Does the agency have their fees clearly stated on their website or on any materials that they send you?
- Do they specialize in a specific type of debt collection, such as medical, retail, credit card, and so on?
- Is the agency prepared to give the best possible service? Though an agency cannot guarantee results on any specific date, they'll often estimate on an average recovery rate that one can expect.
- Will they be sensitive to a consumer's individual situation? The agency should promptly notify you when it discovers a consumer who is a hardship case, and then recommend a proper procedure to follow.

- Does the agency comply with all state laws and federal laws? Have they had any trouble with this in the past?
- Is the agency licensed and bonded and do they have Errors & Omissions insurance?
- How many collectors does the agency have? How many years of experience have they had?
- Has the agency ever been sued? Why? What was the result?
- Can you get recommendations or talk to their past and current clients?

Some agencies offer additional incorporated services such as credit management, accounts receivable outsourcing, and more.

WHEN YOU SHOULD USE A COLLECTION AGENCY

The chances of collecting on an account decrease dramatically as it ages. It's expensive to carry accounts that you will not be able to collect using the methods at your disposal. It therefore becomes a better use of your company's time and resources to concentrate on other aspects of your business. You might do this by hiring a credit manager to do the collection work you have been doing. However, you may then have to place the past-due accounts with an outside or third party collection agency as your business grows. Accordingly, some collection agencies charge more for older accounts because they are harder to collect.

A professional collection service can assist you in gathering money from accounts that remain delinquent. Collectors have a vast knowledge of techniques, technology, and compliance issues. Using a professional service will save time and likely yield better results than you can achieve on your own.

You may want to consider placing accounts with an agency once they reach 90 to 120 days past due. Some people place them at 60 days while some wait more than a year; it is completely up to you. However, keep in mind that the longer you wait, the less your chances are of recovering any of that money.

If you are letting a debt sit on your books and grow older without actively pursuing it, it is worthwhile to give it to a collection agency since nothing is happening with it anyway. Someone else might as well be trying to get your money for you. The following are some indications that you need to place an account with a collection agency:

- A new customer does not respond to the first letter and will not—or cannot—pay for some unknown reason. Potential losses could be kept to a minimum by prompt referral to a collection agency.
- Payment terms fail, or in some cases, irresponsible consumers pay when and if they want to. This group is responsible for 25 to 50 percent of the cost of collections. Cost and potential losses are reduced by quick action.
- The consumer makes repetitious, unfounded complaints. Such consumers are often better handled by a collection agency. You have to decide if dealing with the complaints is worth your time, or would you rather pay an agency a percentage for their time and still receive the money that is due you.
- The consumer totally denies responsibility. Without professional help, these accounts are usually written off as

total losses. This is when it's especially crucial to have a signed credit application or contract as well as proof of the order and who placed it.

- Delinquency coexists with serious marital difficulties. These also require professional collection help, with the added urgency of obtaining payments before the disappearance of one or both of the responsible parties. If both divorced people claim that the other is responsible for the debt, ask for a copy of the divorce decree. This will state which party is responsible.

- Repeat delinquencies occur along with frequent changes of address or jobs. This group is responsible for 90 percent of all "skips"—a consumer who has moved without informing creditors or leaving a forwarding address. Since chances of finding the consumer and collecting a debt diminish over time, taking quick action is especially important here. Most agencies provide a skiptracing or location service; however, be sure to ask if it is included in their fee.

- Obvious financial irresponsibility is apparent. In such cases, little hope exists for voluntary payments and a quick settlement.

It is expensive to carry accounts on your books that you will not be able to collect using only the methods at your disposal. It is often preferable, rather than using your organization's time and resources, to concentrate on other aspects of your business. Depending on your payment terms and in-house collection policies, consider turning the account over to a collection agency for past-due customers who are not responding to you and who are anywhere from 40 to 120 days past-due. Don't drag these out or leave them on your books without taking action. Get rid of them if you can't deal with them in-house in order to get more money collected.

If you have past-due accounts that you are not working on and for which you don't have a signed contract or a paper trail, you might want to write them off and not waste time and money hiring a collection agency. A third party agency is required by law to provide verification of a debt if a debtor requests it, so if you cannot provide the paperwork for a debt, the agency cannot legally collect.

WORKING WITH A COLLECTION AGENCY

Once you've thoroughly researched collection agencies and chosen the one you are going to work with, they will tell you how you can upload accounts to them. Give them as much information as you can to make their job as easy as possible and increase your chance of getting any money. In all cases, the minimum information you provide should include:

- The debtor's correct and full name, address, and contact numbers, including home, cell, work.
- Name of the debtor's spouse, if applicable.
- Let them know if any mail has been returned and why.
- Occupation, last known occupation, spouse's occupation, and phone numbers.
- Names of relatives, friends, neighbors, and references.
- Summary of any disputes.
- Date of last transaction, order, and payment.
- E-mail address and fax number.
- Nicknames or aliases; maiden name.

Much of the above information will be included on the credit application you've had customers fill out, and a summary of any disputes would be in that account's notes. Having all the information that you need in one place or on one piece of paper makes your search easier, which is yet another reason why credit applications are so very important. (I cannot state this enough!) When I ran my collection agency I would have some clients that would place an account with me for collection without any documentation such as a signed credit application, a contract or agreement, a purchase order, a copy of the order, or a proof of delivery. Having documentation for your sales provides a paper trail, thereby giving you the tools you need to get paid. Proper documents allow a collector to have the information needed to effectively collect on an account or pursue it legally. Having a credit application for each customer should be enough. I simply did not accept clients who tried to place accounts with my agency without any documentation, since I would not have any proof of the debt or be able to provide verification if the debtor requested it.

The bottom line is to cooperate with your collection agency in every way possible. Rely on their experience, diligence, and judgment for the best and quickest results, and promptly refer any contact from the debtor to the collection agency. Make sure that your collection agency is familiar with the nature of your goods or services; as mentioned above, some agencies specialize in collecting on specific services. For example, you might find an agency that specializes in delinquent auto loans, or medical bills, or hot tub sales. If you find an agency that specializes in your field, check them out; there is a reason they do only those types of collections.

Another important tip: Do not place any accounts with more than one agency. Make sure that if you decide to change agencies, you remove any accounts from one agency before placing them with another.

Fortunately for you, collection agencies' fees are based on results, not on time spent on the account. However, you cannot expect payments to be made immediately. Remember to refer any contact the debtor makes to the agency once you place an account with them. Your time to work with the debtor has now passed; all correspondence and payments must be conducted through the agency so that they can do their job effectively. Most business owners that place an account with an agency know that it's no longer their place to deal with the debtor, and they have moved on to other things.

HOW COLLECTION AGENCIES GET PAID

The common practice is to pay collection agencies via commission on what is collected. However, not all agencies do this; some may charge a monthly fee or a set fee per letter or contact. When an agency charges a commission, they will normally charge a percentage for "standard" accounts. This would be accounts that are maybe 60 days old, have a good address, phone number, and probably collectable debt. My collection rate was 25 percent of what was collected on "standard" accounts when I had my agency. If an account was under $75 or more than one year old, the percentage was 50 percent of what was collected. Large customers who placed many accounts weekly or monthly would get a special flat rate of 18 percent of what was collected.

Some agencies will charge a flat monthly fee based on the number of accounts you place, how often you place accounts for collection, the dollar amounts, and the age. They may also charge per letter or contact with the debtor. Collection agencies often offer other services at a flat fee, such as skiptracing, credit reporting, or garnishment.

9

Debt Collection Laws, Rules, and Regulations

As a first-party collector you need to follow all state laws in the state where you reside and also the state where your debtor resides. Though we've already discussed some of these state laws, there are some other laws with which you may want to be familiar and keep an eye on, especially since they are changing as of the date of this book's printing. These are:

- CAN-SPAM Act
- Electronic Funds Transfer Act (EFTA)
- FDCPA—Fair Debt Collection Practices Act
- FCRA—Fair Credit Reporting Act
- Gramm-Leach-Bliley Act
- Health Insurance Portability and Accountability Act (HIPAA)
- Red Flags Rule
- Service Members Civil Relief Act
- Telephone Consumer Protection Act
- Truth in Lending Act
- U.S. Bankruptcy Code
- End Debt Collector Abuse Act
- Consumer Financial Protection Act

Business owners and third party collection agencies have to follow different laws. Many company owners are confused about whether they have to follow the Fair Debt Collection Practices Act, which broadly defines a debt collector as "any person who uses any instrument of interstate commerce or the mails in any business the principal purpose of which is the collection of any debts, or who regularly collects or attempts to collect, directly or indirectly, debts owed or due or asserted to be owed or due another." While the FDCPA generally only applies to third party debt collectors—not internal collectors, credit managers for a creditor, or business owners collecting their own debts—some states (such as California) have similar state consumer protection laws that mirror the FDCPA. Therefore, you should be sure to check your state's laws and the laws of the states in which you are collecting.

FDCPA—THE FAIR DEBT COLLECTION PRACTICES ACT

The FDCPA covers the practices of third party collectors and attorneys who regularly collect debts for others. It was created to protect consumers and became effective March 20, 1978. The FDCPA is a federal statute and many states have collection laws that are very similar or the same. Keep in mind that this act was not written for debt collectors but for consumers, in response to outrage by debtors about abusive collection actions during the 1970s. This act helps to provide a defense against third party debt collectors. These laws can also affect business owners who do their own debt collections in-house. Every business owner needs to be familiar with the FDCPA if they extend credit and try to enforce their credit policy. Those who grant credit must know this law because:

- Business owners' collection practices are covered by this law under certain conditions.
- Credit grantors should be aware of what their collection services and attorneys may and may not do under this law.

- Creditors may be liable with respect to the collection practices of third party debt collectors under Section 5 of the Federal Trade Commission Act, and in some cases, under their state laws.
- Credit grantors must comply with FDCPA when they collect their own debts using a name other than their own. For example, if Dunn's Oil Company uses the name The Dunn Collection Service to collect its own debts, they must comply.

Having knowledge of and keeping up to date on the FDCPA will help you maintain structure and follow rules for your credit policy.

The present tough economic times are making it increasingly difficult for small businesses to secure capital and financing. This has caused them to limit or take severe precautions about individuals to whom they decide to extend credit. Without new capital, these fledgling companies are forced to remain very conservative. While this means that they will have fewer problems down the road, they are also more likely to remain stagnant and fail to grow, thereby risking possible failure. In order to break this cycle, lenders need to increase the financing and capital they make available to small business owners to allow them to grow, or even to just stay in business. Unfortunately, this trend seems to be a long way off due to the increasing likelihood of a double-dip recession. Therefore, these owners' only other option is to protect their business and cash flow by limiting credit risk. They can do this by becoming more educated on how to limit their risk.

FDCPA lawsuits are rising each year due to a variety of factors including the economy, media coverage, aggressive consumer attorneys, and consumer websites that tend to encourage lawsuits. It doesn't help that many believe that collecting debts becomes easier because there is more debt out there during a down economy. The fact is that there may be more debt out there, but the economic downturn and outdated laws make it harder to collect. More people may be in debt now than ever before, and many of them have never experienced this. They don't know how to handle it or what their rights or options are. Companies need to be educated so that they can work with these customers in offering a solution, keeping them as customers, and still get paid and limit their credit risk.

The following are some frequently asked questions about the FDCPA.

- Are all debts covered by the FDCPA?

  No, only the collection of consumer debts is covered and regulated by the FDCPA. Business debts are not covered by the FDCPA.

- Who is a "debt collector" under the FDCPA?

  A debt collector is any person who uses mail, the Internet, or the telephone for the principal purpose of collecting a debt; in other words, a person whose job is collecting past-due debts. This also includes anyone who regularly attempts to collect debts owed to someone other than themselves.

  If you are the original creditor, you are not considered a debt collector under the FDCPA. However, you may need to follow any laws of the state where you and/or your debtor/customer are located. If you sell or assign the debt to another person to collect because the debtor is not paying you, that person is not the original creditor and is a debt collector under the act.

There are exceptions to this; for example, the term debt collector under the FDCPA includes any original creditor who is trying to collect their own debt and is using a different name, which indicates a third party is trying to collect. This can include lawyers, law firms, landlords, or homeowner associations.

- Can I call a debtor at work?

  Yes, unless they tell you that it is inconvenient for them to receive calls at work or that their employer doesn't allow them to receive debt collection or personal calls at work. This can be done verbally and does not need to be in writing.

- Can I ask a neighbor, spouse, or parent to give the debtor a message?

  No, you cannot ask anyone to give the debtor a message about a debt. You can discuss the debt only with the debtor or a cosigner who may be responsible for the debt.

  The Fair Debt Collection Practices Act seeks to eliminate debt collection abuse and helps good debt collectors while protecting consumers or debtors as well as creditors. The law imposes restrictions on various practices for the collection of debts by an independent third party or a collection agency. Debt collectors are allowed to contact a debtor in these ways:

- In person
- By mail
- By telephone
- By telegram
- By fax

Agencies are restricted from contacting debtors at inconvenient times or places. They are also prohibited from contacting debtors at their place of employment if the agency is aware that the debtor's employer disapproves of this action. Debt collection agencies are additionally prohibited from certain harassing or abusive practices.

The FDCPA regulates consumer debt, which it defines as "any obligation or alleged obligation of a consumer to pay money arising out of a transaction in which the money, property, insurance, or services which are the subject of the transaction are primarily for personal, family, or household purposes, whether or not such obligation has been reduced to judgment. This can include purchases of an automobile, for medical care, or any charge account." As mentioned above, business debts are not regulated by the FDCPA.

Although the FDCPA offers some protections, it only applies under certain circumstances:

- The debt must be a consumer debt.
- The collector cannot be the original creditor.

The FDCPA broadly defines a debt collector as "any person who uses any instrumentality of interstate commerce or the mails in any business the principal purpose of which is the collection of any debts, or who regularly collects or attempts to collect, directly or indirectly, debts owed or due or asserted to be owed or due another." While the FDCPA generally only applies to third-party debt collectors—not internal collectors for an "original creditor"—some states, such as California, have similar state consumer protection laws that mirror the FDCPA and regulate original creditors. In addition, courts have generally found debt buyers to be covered by the

FDCPA even though they are collecting their own debts. The definitions and coverage have changed over time. The FDCPA itself contains numerous exceptions to the definition of a "debt collector," particularly after the October 13, 2006, passage of the Financial Services Regulatory Relief Act of 2006. Attorneys, originally explicitly excepted from the definition of a debt collector, have been included (to the extent that they otherwise meet the definition) since 1986. Original creditors do not have to follow the FDCPA but must follow state laws.

It's important to point out that you are doing the right thing in trying to learn more about the FDCPA and educating yourself. It's also vital to keep in mind while making collection calls or sending letters that the table could be turned at any moment. You could find yourself in financial trouble and you could be the debtor. How would you feel? How would you react to a bill collector? If you can put yourself in the position of the person on the receiving end of your correspondence or call, you'll do a better job, follow the law, and collect more money.

While the FDCPA does state that "unfair" practices are banned, they do not specifically define the term "unfair." Some examples of "unfair" might be:

- Indicating that you are a debt collector or work for a collection agency on the outside of an envelope or anything mailed to the debtor.
- Communicating via postcard.
- Collecting more than the amount that is legally due.
- Accepting a post-dated check, unless you notify the writer of the check your intent to deposit the check not

more than 10 or less than three business days prior to your depositing the check.

- Soliciting a post-dated check with the intent of criminal prosecution.
- Depositing or threatening to deposit a post-dated check before the date indicated on the check.
- Placing collect phone calls to the debtor.
- Sending telegrams to the debtor at their expense.
- Causing injury to a debtor.
- Making contact when you know it is inconvenient to the debtor.
- Making contact before 8 A.M. and after 9 P.M. local time unless you have special permission.

It is also important to be aware of potential FDCPA violations. One of these might be making false or misleading representations in communications with the consumer or debtor, via either phone calls, letters, and/or voice mail messages. Another would be to give a false impression as to the amount of the debt or the legal status of that debt, while another would be to convey the false impression that you as the collector are an attorney, a credit reporting agency, or are affiliated with the federal or a state government. In fact, giving the false impression that you as the collector are going to pursue some type of action that is illegal would be a violation—for example, implying that nonpayment will result in arrest when an arrest in those circumstances would be illegal. Threatening legal action when you cannot or have no intention of pursuing legal action would be a violation as well; for example, you cannot state or send a letter to the debtor saying that a lawsuit will be filed if payment is not received within seven days.

Another violation would be giving the debtor the false impression that they have committed a crime by failing to pay their debt. If a collector uses any false, deceptive, or misleading representation in regards to debt collection that I have not mentioned here, the FDCPA will most likely still offer the consumer protection from it. *Be careful*!

There is a "good faith" defense in any FDCPA suit. To be able to claim this, you should reduce your risk with these tips.

- Undergo debt collection training. You can never do too much of this!
- Make collectors aware that their actions or inactions could create financial headaches personally and for the business owner.
- Monitor your employees and test them periodically.
- Fire employees who don't comply with the FDCPA.
- Retain a FDCPA attorney in your area.
- Read and reread the act, and make copies available for all your collectors.
- Be clear on state laws, both where you are collecting and where you are located.
- Keep accurate and detailed records in case you need to produce them in court.

FCRA—THE FAIR CREDIT REPORTING ACT

The Fair Credit Reporting Act (FCRA) is enforced by the Federal Trade Commission and was designed to promote accuracy and ensure the privacy of the information used in consumer credit reports. Originally passed in 1970, this law ensures that consumers have access to information about them that lenders, insurers, and others obtain from credit bureaus and use to make decisions about providing credit and other services. The FCRA also requires that users of credit reports have a "permissible purpose" to obtain them. It also mandates that credit reporting agencies maintain the security and integrity of consumer files, and allows consumers to limit certain uses of their reports. Your "permissible purpose" would be to extend credit—thus the importance —of having a signed credit application.

There are rules and laws you must follow when you decide to report debtors' credit history to any of the credit bureaus. FCRA violations can lead to both civil and criminal penalties. Civil penalties, including nominal damages, actual damages, punitive damages, and attorneys' fees and costs, may apply where there is willful noncompliance with the Act. Civil penalties for negligent noncompliance are restricted to actual damages and attorneys' fees and costs. Criminal penalties may apply where an individual knowingly and willfully obtains information from a consumer reporting agency under false pretenses.

Employers and business owners who fail to give the appropriate notices or obtain authorization may be sued by affected individuals. Consumer reporting agencies and users of consumer information who willfully or negligently fail to comply with any requirement imposed under the FCRA may be liable for actual damages, court costs, and reasonable attorneys' fees. Punitive damages also are available for willful violations. In addition, the FTC may sue employers for civil penalties of not more than $2,500 per violation.

You can report to one, two, or all three of the credit bureaus, which are:

1. Equifax
   P.O. Box 740241
   Atlanta, GA 30374
   888-202-4025
   www.equifax.com
2. Experian
   888-243-6951
   www.experian.com
3. TransUnion
   P.O. Box 2000
   Chester, PA 19022
   www.transunion.com

WHAT LAWS ARE CHANGING AND HOW IT AFFECTS YOU

The laws that govern the debt collection industry are enforced by the Federal Trade Commission (FTC). Recently, the FTC has been analyzing the laws governing debt collection and is working on updating them. We are hopeful that, as the FDCPA is updated and changes are made, online collection techniques and technology will be specifically addressed.

The Federal Trade Commission has concluded that the current system for resolving consumer debts is broken. To repair it, they have set forth a variety of significant reforms that federal and state governments, the debt collection industry, and others need to make for the system to be both efficient and fair.

Changes made to the FDCPA do not affect you as a business owner or a credit manager collecting your own debts. What does affect you is any state or federal laws that may be changed and you would then have to follow. These laws are important to mention even if you don't have to follow them; it simply makes good business for you to be aware of what they are. If they are changed in the future and end up affecting you, you will be ahead of the game by becoming familiar with them now.

THE END DEBT COLLECTOR ABUSE ACT

The End Debt Collector Abuse Act is a new Act (S.3888), which has been introduced to help amend the FDCPA. This proposed legislation would require third party debt collectors or collection agencies to include basic information—such as last payment date, the total amount of the debt, documentation of the principal amount, interest and any fees, information for the consumer on their rights under the law, and contact information for the consumer who may have complaints about the collector—in their debt validation notices. It would also mandate that collection agencies now be responsible for investigating and helping to resolve disputed debts; this was not up to the collector in the past. This act should help to deter bad behavior from third party collectors and lessen consumer abuse from unscrupulous collectors that don't follow the law. It can only help those of us who do follow the law and are not abusive towards consumers—but are just trying to do our job as bill collectors.

THE CONSUMER FINANCIAL PROTECTION ACT

On July 21, 2010, President Obama signed into law the Dodd-Frank Wall Street Reform and Consumer Protection Act. This Act establishes a Bureau of Consumer Financial Protection that will assume broad regulatory powers over debt collectors and all other persons who have any connection to consumer finance or services. This Bureau will have exclusive rule making or enforcement authority with respect to any Federal statutes that impact the debt collection industry, including the FDCPA and the FCRA. The Act will cover third party bill collectors, including collection attorneys, anyone who is extending credit and servicing loans, as well as service providers to debt collectors. The purpose of this new Bureau is to assure that consumers are treated fairly.

HOW FINANCIAL REFORM AFFECTS YOUR BUSINESS

The financial reform bill is supposed to keep what has happened on Wall Street from happening again. President Obama claims that the new bill will provide economic security to families and businesses. He has stated that it ensures that there will be no more taxpayer bailouts and that Wall Street will be responsible for its own actions.

Many Americans are still dealing with the recession with no end in sight—for themselves personally or for business owners. This bill can only help us move forward instead of going backwards to where we were before the crash. It is Congress's attempt to respond to a financial disaster—and without any other options, the best approach for all of us would be to try to understand this bill and how it will affect us. It is supposed to reflect progress and change in our financial markets, which should be good news for small business owners. Right now, small businesses seem to be paying the highest price for a financial crisis they did not create.

There are several things business owners should be aware of with the passing of this bill. One is that if you applied and were rejected for a loan or were denied a lease, you can get a free copy of your credit score from the three credit bureaus. Your credit score is the number on your credit report that strongly indicates how likely you are to pay back a loan, mortgage, or any debt based on your borrowing and payment history. The higher your score, the more likely lenders assume that you will pay them back. Your credit score is used by a lender to determine the type of loan and amount of credit you qualify for, as well as what your interest rate will be. This new bill will allow creditors to acquire a free copy of their credit score; this way, they'll know before going to a lender what they might qualify for. They can find out whether they need to work on their score a bit more in order to approach a lender for a loan, and they might even have some leeway in negotiating an interest rate with a good score. Scores range from 300 to 740, with 740 being an excellent credit score, and anything below 620 considered poor. You'll want to monitor your score and try to get it up above 620 or higher in order to get the best loans with the best interest rates.

Another aspect of this bill is that the mortgage industry will also be changing—something that can affect your company if you have a mortgage in your company's name. There will now be mandatory verification for mortgages; in other words, your lender will be required to fully document your income when you apply for a mortgage. Though this might seem incredibly simple or common sense, it was something that frequently was not being done. The lender will also need to verify that you will be able to pay back the loan before approving you. The bill will also prevent lenders from offering incentives to mortgage brokers, especially if they are trying to sell loans with unreasonable interest rates, something that many had done in the past. One especially attractive element of this bill is that it will be the end of prepayment penalties. This means that you can now pay off your loan early without suffering consequences for it!

There are a few things to look out for, however. Some experts think that due to all these new changes, it may be harder to obtain a loan at all, since the banks will not be making as much money as in the past. This seems a little crazy to me; after all, aren't banks in business to make loans? Now that they have rules to follow and can't slap borrowers with all kinds of hidden fees, they don't want to loan us money? This is actually the worst time for this to happen; it's already close to impossible to obtain a loan. This might make it harder with even more red tape.

This bill will bring many changes for consumers and companies all over the United States. One of these is that the government will now have the power to break up a company that is struggling if it will threaten the economy should it fail. Many news channels are reporting that even though this bill has passed, it might take up to two years for all of these changes to go into effect. While this bill isn't going to make everyone happy, few things rarely do. But it is better than nothing, and certainly an improvement over the problems of the past!

How many small business owners do you think will survive the next five years? Will your business fall by the wayside and be replaced with one of the many new organizations being launched every day? Of course you don't want this to happen, and there are several things you can do in order to survive and thrive in these tough times. One of these things is looking at your company's structure. Start to organize and manage your business in a way that helps you meet today's challenges. Try to step away from hard rules, policies, or procedures that may not even be working anymore, and attempt to work with people who have experience and know what is going on in the financial arena. Begin to cross-train your employees by having your credit department train with the sales department or your operations or inventory control train with marketing and customer service. (You should be doing this anyway!) Exposing everyone within your company to departments other than their own can only help your business flow more smoothly. Everyone will know what everyone else is doing as well as what they can do to help make each other's jobs easier and more effective. This will increase your efficiency, which will be reflected in your bottom line.

Meet with your employees and ask them how to achieve the goals you want to accomplish. They know better than you; after all, they do this job every day. Confirm that your employees have all the tools they need to do their job. Ask them questions and include them in decisions. Make sure that you're all working towards the same goals. This will not only increase your profits, it improves employee morale, and we all know that happy employees lead to a happy company that makes money.

Though many of the issues concerning reform might seem confusing, there are things that you as a business owner can do. Ask questions, review your own business plan, and try to make it through this financial crisis as best you can. Though our financial systems are flawed, it is slightly comforting to know that our government is attempting to find ways to fix it.

BANKRUPTCY

There are three types of bankruptcy:
1. Chapter 13—Wage earners: adjustment of debt or an individual with regular income
2. Chapter 11—Business reorganization
3. Chapter 7—Total liquidation

On April 20, 2005, President Bush signed into law the Bankruptcy Abuse Prevention and Consumer Protection Act of 2005. The BAPCPA has an impact on all small business owners, and there are several things you can do to protect your company. Pay attention to your accounts receivables; you should review all accounts and keep an eye on your larger ones regularly. If you are a very small business that loses a single, large-sized account due to a bankruptcy filing, this can upset your cash flow, so you want to know that this is coming before it hits you. One way is to be aware of the warning signs that someone is close to filing bankruptcy, such as a slow payer who suddenly places a large order. Customers who are anticipating financial trouble might try to stock up on your goods or services in advance. If this happens, ask for a portion of the payment up front or ask that their balance be paid in full before you process another order.

The BAPCPA can help you by making it easier to defend against a preference claim. This law requires that any lawsuit or preference claim for less than $10,000 must be filed in the area where your business is located, rather than in the city where the bankruptcy case or the customer is located. A preference claim is a claim seeking to recover specific payments that were made by the debtor prior to the bankruptcy filing. This could be a payment made by the debtor to a creditor within 90 days of filing bankruptcy or when the debtor was insolvent. Preference claims are intended to promote the Bankruptcy Code's equality of distribution of funds among creditors in similar situations. Bankruptcy law, as drafted by Congress, feels it is unfair if one creditor was paid within 90 days of a debtor filing for bankruptcy when other similar creditors were not. This is great news for your company, because you will not have to incur any costs by traveling or hiring an attorney in another state to defend the claim.

The BAPCPA also makes it easier for an organization to defend itself against a preference claim by eliminating the need to prove that the alleged preference payment was made in accord with industry standards. The law makes it so that the company only needs to prove that the payments were made in the ordinary course of events between the business and the bankrupt consumer or company. The BAPCPA also gives you and your company 45 days to send a written demand for the return of your shipped goods if a customer files bankruptcy.

DEATH

When a customer that owes you money dies, their debts are paid out of their estate, if they have one. Though not everyone will have an estate, many people do. It is usually comprised of their money, including anything from insurance, property, investments, and possessions. Normally, when someone dies and there is not a will, someone, usually a relative is appointed as the estate's executor or administrator. A spouse is not automatically responsible for a spouse's debts, unless both names were on the note, they had a joint loan, or they provided a loan guarantee of some kind.

If there are debts owed at the time of a customer's death, the estate will pay them off in a specific order before any money goes to anyone listed in the will. Personal loans or credit cards are usually paid last and, many times, there is no money left for these types of bills.

If you have many accounts in which you have extended credit to elderly customers, death might be an area of concern for you. Fortunately, there are some precautions you can take.

- Require two names on each account.
- Keep credit limits lower to reduce your risk.
- Only offer credit on one order at a time; this means that customers pay for one order before they can charge another one.
- Contact your insurance company to see if there are benefits to cover such situations.

Once a customer dies and you make a call to inquire about payment on an account, you want to ask the following questions:

- Is there insurance?
- Who is the insurance company, and what is their phone number?
- Who is handling the estate?

SKIPTRACING

Skiptracing takes place when you are trying to locate a customer that owes you money but has a disconnected phone, mail that has been returned, and you are unable to get in touch with them. Some things you can do to locate a debtor who has skipped town are:

- Google them.
- Call the old phone number; sometimes there will be a recording listing the new number.
- Look them up in the white pages, either online or in your hard copy of the phone book.
- Pull a credit report if you have permission (via a signed credit application).
- Use an online service such as Accurint or Search America.
- If they have a Facebook or other social networking page, check to see if there is a work number or name of the company they work for; then look up the business's website to get a phone number.
- Go to the local courthouse and look up public records, or do it online.

AN IN-DEPTH LOOK AT SKIPTRACING BY RON BROWN, A PROFESSIONAL SKIPTRACER AND THE AUTHOR OF THE BOOK *MANHUNT*

Professional Skiptracers in the twenty-first century must possess many advanced communication skills. Many are fully knowledgeable of the current technology available to help them be successful in their endeavors. Combined with neuro-linguistic skills, this advanced technology has produced an advanced skiptracing process commonly referred to as "Triangulation Tracing." This technique is a combination of "Cybertracking" and "Skiptracing," and is becoming common in the credit and collection industry.

This tracing method starts with a "Batch Search" and is a very effective way to start the tracing process. The system uses electronic file transfers to "wash" files through various data banks, looking for matches that provide new or additional information. All of the major data resellers will provide this service on a "no hit/no fee" basis at a very fair price.

The second part of "Triangulation Tracing" takes place when the search is continued by a "Cybertracker"—an individual who handles this part of the tracing process. Cybertrackers must be extremely computer literate, know where pertinent data is stored, as well as how to access and interpret any received data. It is important that they explore the advantages and disadvantages of using free data sites, in addition to familiarizing themselves with the data brokers who gather and resell information. Tracers are also required to be a member of and understand the techniques used to navigate social sites such as MySpace, Facebook, and Twitter. These sites are growing rapidly and expanding into other areas such as to business sites like LinkedIn and education institution sites such as Alumni.com and Classmates.com.

Cybertrackers are a relatively new breed of tracers. Because they never speak to anyone, they have the ability to trace at any time of the day or night and require a limited amount of training. The use of Cybertrackers in first party tracing is becoming a common occurrence in the credit and collection industry.

The third and final stage of Triangulation Tracing requires the efforts of a professional tracer.

This tracer must endeavor to speak with a voice that is friendly but that conveys a bit of urgency. They must like to interact with others and speak with a sense of warmth, which exudes confidence and trust.

The tracer must possess not only excellent communication skills but must also have a good ear. This developed ear helps the tracer not only hear what is said but also hear and recognize what is *not* said—and interpret the true meaning of both. Often, it's what customers are not saying—or the way they phrase their statements—that provides the tracer with the final clue that enables them to locate their subject.

Finally, a professional tracer must be able to think and reason as the person they are hunting thinks, reasons, and moves. Tracers have knowledge of how far the person they are tracing will go to prevent being located, and the tracer must be willing to travel that same path. They must understand "backwards tracing"—the process of going backwards in your trace process to the point where you know for sure where the person you are tracking was at a particular time. You then move forward looking for patterns and habits until you are able to actually move in front of and intercept your subject.

Once tracers have mastered these primary skills, they're prepared to embark on one of the most rewarding and exciting aspects of the collection and recovery industry: the true skiptracing process.

It is imperative as they develop these skills that they build a good network of both open and closed sources of information. These contacts will prove invaluable as they proceed to hone their expertise. It's always a good idea to use business cards to build a network, both by giving them out to others and filing away those that people distribute. It's also smart to write on the back of each individual's card the date and place the person was met, as well as a personal detail about them. That provides you with a relationship comment when you have to contact them for information, thus increasing the chance for success.

There's one final thing that those who proceed on the exciting path of becoming a professional tracer must have. The ability of man to trace throughout history has always paralleled the ability to communicate—and never before have we possessed the communication skills and tools that we have today. There's never been as much information and data so readily available to which we're able to apply tracing analytics as accurately as we do today. It is vital that we embrace this technology as we continue to develop our personal communication skills—and never forget the greatest and most powerful tool a tracer possesses is his or her human mind.

LOCATING AND TRACKING CUSTOMERS USING SOCIAL MEDIA

Consumers everywhere are upset that collectors are utilizing social networks to locate them in order to collect a debt. Many are calling it unethical and just another "low life tactic" to harass a debtor. It's critical to remember that debtors are in the positions they're in because they owe someone money. Unfortunately, many debtors think that if their financial situation changes or they overspend, they should no longer have to pay off their debts —and are upset when they are asked to do that. They might feel differently if they were the business owners who sold someone their product but never got paid.

On September 28, 2009, the *New York Daily News* ran a story by Tripp Whetsell entitled "Collection firms join old pals looking for you on Facebook." The article told the tale of Michael Bucello, an individual who got his first credit card when he was in college and who then had trouble resisting the urge to use the card for his purchases. He racked up over $1,600 in charges on his card, had trouble paying—and shredded the card but never paid the debt. Bucello's reason for failing to pay was that he had received several notices about the past due balance, but then presumed as the years went by that his old debts had been forgotten.

This is a common story and excuse from debtors. Many assume that if they just ignore a debt, it will go away. But obviously, a bill you don't pay is still out there. Bucello expressed irritation that a debt collector noticed his Facebook page, prompting collection activities to resume. However, he decided to make good on his debt when his bank account was frozen. He did go on to say that he is a lot more vigilant now about what he does on the Internet, and that he also got a crash course about the importance of paying his bills on time.

Technological advancement allows social media to be used by skiptracers, business owners, or debt collectors to obtain, verify, and analyze information regarding their customers. *The Associated Press* also reported recently that Facebook will save user profiles of deceased people. This means if you are looking for a deceased debtor and find their Facebook profile, you will instead see a memorial profile. Though Facebook will delete contact information from memorial profiles and block people from logging into the deceased person's account, you can use this information to close out an account or pursue the estate once you verify that the person is deceased.

Additionally, the Internal Revenue Service in a few states has a new tool in social media as well. According to a report in the *Wall Street Journal*, authorities in Minnesota, Nebraska, California, and several other states mine information from Facebook and MySpace and have been able to successfully collect back taxes. They look for a wide variety of information to help them collect, such as relocation announcements, earnings boasts, gig notices, and more.

I recently read that a Nebraska tax official named Steven Schroeder indicated to the *Wall Street Journal* that using a Google search is often the first step when the IRS can't find a tax evader. If a Google search doesn't return any results, they visit social network sites and online chat rooms. Spokespeople for some states, including Wisconsin and Oregon, indicated they are actively looking into these methods, and many other states are considering using social media for tax audits, negotiations, and collections. Some collection attorneys or process servers claim to have used the pictures people post on Facebook or MySpace to help them get a physical description of persons so they can serve them with legal paperwork.

Conclusion

Good collectors can convey the kind of urgency to a customer that results in an action being taken. Some collectors stand apart; they grab more attention, close more deals, and persuade more customers to send in payments. You can easily be one of those collectors.

A good strategy to follow is to pretend you are talking to someone younger than you when you make a collection call; always keep it straightforward and to the point. Speaking in clear and simple terms will bring you better results. Create and articulate your vision: to collect the money that is owed to you.

Listen carefully, and consider all feedback. One of the most effective actions you can take to achieve success as a collector is to listen. Listen enough to show compassion and understand the situation, but don't lose control of the call or get stuck listening to someone's woes for hours.

Review and practice your impending interaction. Go over your customer's account thoroughly before you pick up the phone to call. Rehearse in your head what you will say in each particular situation. Be ready for every excuse and personify confidence.

Remember to be reasonable and appreciate the fact that not all customers will be able to pay in full when you call. Listen, be confident, ask for the full amount—and then listen again to their response. Devise a payment plan that works for the customer but benefits your company as well.

Always attempt to be as comprehensible as possible. Deliver financial information using concise and direct language. Good business communicators use simple language to discuss complex issues.

Give praise and remember to show gratitude. When a customer makes good on a payment promise, send a letter thanking them for it. This acknowledges that you received the payment, tells them the new lower balance, and gives them some attention. If a customer sends in a payment and hears nothing, they may not send another one. As with anything, a little courtesy goes a long way.

Above all, treat your customers with dignity and respect. Don't look down on a customer that is past-due; remember, that could be you. Anyone can find themselves in a situation where they are unable to pay their bills. Be a professional and treat everyone fairly and with respect. If you don't do this you will lose any chance of collecting money and your business will lose customers. Being ethical when trying to do a difficult job is a necessity.

Making collection calls might not be the most fun and exciting task out there, but it is incredibly necessary. After all, you are helping to make sure that something essential to business takes place: that people get paid for the jobs they've done! So do yours with a sense of pride. Be positive, upbeat, and enthusiastic. Your task is to get the person on the other end of the phone to feel good about sending you money towards their bill, and about how you are going to help make that happen.

Approach your interactions with a bill collector attitude—one that is positive about collecting money. Set a goal based on the accounts you will be contacting and see if you can reach that goal by the end of the day or week. This gives you some incentive to do a good job and stay motivated—and to continue doing your job to the best of your ability.

About the Author

Michelle Dunn is an award winning author of 17 books, a successful businesswoman, a columnist, and an internationally known expert on the topic of credit and collections. Michelle is a New York Book Festival winner, a Best Books Award finalist, one of the Top 5 Women in Collections for two consecutive years, one of the Top 50 most influential collection professionals, and the recipient of a Business Excellence Award. Her books include *Getting Paid Using Social Media, Mosquito Marketing for Authors, Using Social Media in Collections, The Ultimate Credit and Collections Handbook, Effective Collections: A Proactive Approach to Credit Management, Online Collection Techniques: Do's and Don'ts, Establishing Payment Arrangements: Beyond Net 30, Understanding and Following the Fair Debt Collection Practices Act, Understanding Identity Theft, FAQ's on Starting a Collection Agency, Starting a Business with Michelle Dunn—Book 1, A Collection Guide for Creditors, Starting a Collection Agency, How to Make Money Collecting Money, 3rd edition, How to Get Your Customers to Pay, Fast, Easy, Effective Letters, How to Help You Get Paid, Credit & Collection Forms and Letters, The*

First Book of Effective Collection Agency Letters and Forms, and *Become the Squeaky Wheel*. Dunn has co-authored and contributed to *Shameless Marketing for Brazen Hussies* with Marilyn Ross; *Home Based Business for Dummies* with Paul and Sarah Edwards and Peter Economy, *Successful Meetings* with Shri Henkel; and *365 Foolish Mistakes Smart Managers Make Every Day* with Shri Henkel. She has also contributed to the Woman's Advantage Calendar each year for the last five years. Michelle recently wrote the foreword for a book being published by Atlantic Publishing called *How to Own and Operate a Financially Successful Collection Agency*, by Emonica Dames.

Michelle is an avid reader, writer, gardener, and boxer. She lives in New Hampshire with her family.

INDEX